Donald Buresh

Customer Satisfaction and Agile Methods

Donald Buresh

Customer Satisfaction and Agile Methods

Assessing Customer Satisfaction and Agile Project Management Methods

VDM Verlag Dr. Müller

Impressum/Imprint (nur für Deutschland/ only for Germany)

Bibliografische Information der Deutschen Nationalbibliothek: Die Deutsche Nationalbibliothek verzeichnet diese Publikation in der Deutschen Nationalbibliografie; detaillierte bibliografische Daten sind im Internet über http://dnb.d-nb.de abrufbar.

Alle in diesem Buch genannten Marken und Produktnamen unterliegen warenzeichen-, marken- oder patentrechtlichem Schutz bzw. sind Warenzeichen oder eingetragene Warenzeichen der jeweiligen Inhaber. Die Wiedergabe von Marken, Produktnamen, Gebrauchsnamen, Handelsnamen, Warenbezeichnungen u.s.w. in diesem Werk berechtigt auch ohne besondere Kennzeichnung nicht zu der Annahme, dass solche Namen im Sinne der Warenzeichen- und Markenschutzgesetzgebung als frei zu betrachten wären und daher von jedermann benutzt werden dürften.

Coverbild: www.purestockx.com

Verlag: VDM Verlag Dr. Müller Aktiengesellschaft & Co. KG
Dudweiler Landstr. 125 a, 66123 Saarbrücken, Deutschland
Telefon +49 681 9100-698, Telefax +49 681 9100-988, Email: info@vdm-verlag.de
Zugl.: Prescott Valley, Northcentral University, Dissertation, 2008

Herstellung in Deutschland:
Schaltungsdienst Lange o.H.G., Zehrensdorfer Str. 11, D-12277 Berlin
Books on Demand GmbH, Gutenbergring 53, D-22848 Norderstedt
Reha GmbH, Dudweiler Landstr. 99, D- 66123 Saarbrücken
ISBN: 978-3-639-09476-3

Imprint (only for USA, GB)

Bibliographic information published by the Deutsche Nationalbibliothek: The Deutsche Nationalbibliothek lists this publication in the Deutsche Nationalbibliografie; detailed bibliographic data are available in the Internet at http://dnb.d-nb.de.

Any brand names and product names mentioned in this book are subject to trademark, brand or patent protection and are trademarks or registered trademarks of their respective holders. The use of brand names, product names, common names, trade names, product descriptions etc. even without
a particular marking in this works is in no way to be construed to mean that such names may be regarded as unrestricted in respect of trademark and brand protection legislation and could thus be used by anyone.

Cover image: www.purestockx.com

Publisher:
VDM Verlag Dr. Müller Aktiengesellschaft & Co. KG
Dudweiler Landstr. 125 a, 66123 Saarbrücken, Germany
Phone +49 681 9100-698, Fax +49 681 9100-988, Email: info@vdm-verlag.de

Copyright © 2008 VDM Verlag Dr. Müller Aktiengesellschaft & Co. KG and licensors
All rights reserved. Saarbrücken 2008

Produced in USA and UK by:
Lightning Source Inc., 1246 Heil Quaker Blvd., La Vergne, TN 37086, USA
Lightning Source UK Ltd., Chapter House, Pitfield, Kiln Farm, Milton Keynes, MK11 3LW, GB
BookSurge, 7290 B. Investment Drive, North Charleston, SC 29418, USA
ISBN: 978-3-639-09476-3

DEDICATION

First and foremost, this study is dedicated to Frannie Umek, Cody, Heidi, and Poofie whose constant friendship, humor, faith, and belief in me are precious and invaluable. This work is also dedicated to my eighth grade teacher, Gloria Range, who gently showed me many years ago that life is all about dreams.

ACKNOWLEDGEMENT

I thank Srini Raghavan who suggested the dissertation topic, and Grayson Walker who lent me a helping hand along the way. During my time at Northcentral University, I have had six academic advisors, including Billie Alarie, Kathy Thoreson, Judy Segner, Rita Ferencak, Freda Turner, and Tina Clicquot Mack. Without the help from these individuals, I would never have completed my dissertation. I thank Richard Bergstrom who constantly reminded me that earning a doctorate was a medieval process, and that jumping through hoops was normal. Jack Aschkenazi, Marta Leonida, Omari Martin, Barbara Parks, and Victoria Schoedel are my very dear friends who were always there for me, particularly when I had specific questions that demanded answers, or just wanted to talk. I thank Deepa Kumar who always responded to my many telephone calls when I had statistical questions, and Norma Turner who advised me regarding APA citation and formatting. I especially thank Sheila Schmitz who was an awesome dissertation advisor, and deserves a very special thank you. I acknowledge the help from Robert Haussmann, Vijay Kanabar, Jaime Klein, and Daljit Singh whose insight brought me great rewards. The 185 nameless individuals who were courageous enough to provide me with data are thanked most kindly, for without them the research would not have gone forward. Finally, I acknowledge that any errors in this dissertation are mine and mine alone. I did my best, and I hope that I have extended the body of human knowledge in some small way, for it has always been the goal of my life.

TABLE OF CONTENTS

LIST OF TABLES

LIST OF FIGURES

CHAPTER 1 - INTRODUCTION

Statement of the Problem

The focus of this quantitative dissertation was to examine whether the use and results of agile-driven software development methods satisfy customers more than the use and results of plan-driven software development methods. The purpose of the research was to investigate whether there is a statistically significant difference in customer satisfaction when a project manager employed agile-driven software development methods rather than plan-driven software development methods. A statistical examination was required because both technologies purport to satisfy customers over and above the customers involved in software development projects employing other technologies. What was evident from a study of the literature was that little or no research had been conducted substantiating this claim (Cao, 2005; Cao, 2006).

Background and Significance of the Problem

Agile-driven methods are a response to the fact that most software development projects are managed poorly, resulting in significant cost overruns and serious delays in the delivery of the final product (Highsmith, 2004). One of the more fruitful process-oriented methodologies is Goldratt's (1990) Theory of Constraints, where the challenge was to translate Goldratt's techniques to software engineering and other computer-related fields (Anderson, 2004). The issue is that many of the salient features of the theory could be lost when superimposing it on a software development process (Boehm & Turner, 2004). Boehm and Turner (2004) believed that software engineering practices are at times cryptic and do not readily lend themselves to the imposition of practices from other industries.

It is not that software development and software engineering are uncontrollable processes; but rather, the purported power of agile-driven methods is that it permits a project manager to focus on responding to and achieving value quickly (Boehm & Turner, 2004). The value of agile-driven software development methods is in the understanding of what variables can be tracked, and what variables can be safely ignored, so that appropriate and timely information is available to customers and senior management.

The *Agile Manifesto* is a simple declaration consisting of 12 principles (Beck, Beedle, van Bennekum, Cockburn, Cunningham, Fowler et al., 2001). The principles were designed to generate software in a timely manner, building a project around motivated individuals, conveying information effectively, maximizing the amount of work done, and most importantly, satisfying the customer. Although the goals of the manifesto seem to be commendable, it may be that only marginal results can be obtained in practice because the field is in a state of apparent flux (Boehm & Turner, 2004). According to Anderson (2004), agile-driven methods for software development projects are essentially a methodology for applying the Theory of Constraints to achieve the desired business results. Thus, it seems that the Theory of Constraints may be directly applicable to software development projects, where the focus is on maximizing throughput, while minimizing operating expenses and inventory (Goldratt, 1990; Anderson, 2004). The translation of these process-oriented concepts to software development is however fraught with some risk, because software developers may find the imposition of the methodology to be unwarranted (Anderson, 2004).

The Project Management Institute has also developed and promoted a body of knowledge on project management, where a project is run employing a bottom-up approach. Detailed descriptions of project activities, or work breakdown structures, are formulated typically at the beginning of the project with the hope that the work breakdown structure remains viscous throughout the course of a project, and that changes occur when cause can be clearly shown (PMBOK Guide, 2005).

The research in this dissertation was used to assess whether the use and results agile-driven software development methodologies are as effective in satisfying customers as the use and results of plan-driven software development methodologies. Christensen (1997) suggested that the reason projects fail is because the customary answers of planning better, working harder, and becoming more customer driven actually exacerbate the problem. The whole purpose of plan-driven project management techniques is to capture and satisfy customer needs at the beginning of a project. Thus, agile-driven methodologies may be better able to address the needs of the customers throughout a project, thereby ensuring its continued success.

One of the major goals of agile-driven methods is the incorporation of customer input to ensure timely delivery of software products (Beck et al., 2001). The focus is on satisfying the customer throughout the software development cycle. In contrast, in plan-driven software development methodologies, the customer reviews the progress of the software being developed either at pre-established milestones or at the end of the project (Desaulniers & Anderson, 2001). The difference in customer involvement is critical, and leads directly to the statement of the problem that was examined in this study.

Research Question

The research question guiding the study was: What is the difference, if any, in customer satisfaction between the use and results of agile-driven software development methods and the use and results of plan-driven software development software development methods? The data were analyzed to explore the following hypotheses:

H0:   The autonomous customer satisfaction for a project using agile-driven software development methods is equal to the autonomous customer satisfaction for a project using plan-driven software development methods.

$H1_a$:   The autonomous customer satisfaction for a project using agile-driven software development methods is greater than the autonomous customer satisfaction for a project using plan-driven software development methods.

$H1_b$:   The autonomous customer satisfaction for a project using plan-driven software development methods is greater than the autonomous customer satisfaction for a project using agile-driven software development methods.

The statistical procedure examined if H0 and $H1_b$ could be rejected at the 95% or 99% confidence levels. If so, it would mean that autonomous customer satisfaction for projects using agile-driven software development methods was significantly greater than autonomous customer satisfaction for projects using plan-driven software development methods. The research regressed customer satisfaction, the dependent variable, against product quality, project team effectiveness, and project management effectiveness, the three independent variables. A dummy variable was added to the regression equation, where the dummy variable equaled zero for plan-driven software development projects, and equaled one for agile-driven software development projects.

Definition of Terms

The four variables, or key terms, that are defined herein include customer satisfaction, the dependent variable, and product quality, project team effectiveness, and project management effectiveness, the three independent variables.

Customer Satisfaction

Varva (1997) viewed customer satisfaction as either an *outcome* or a *process*. The outcome portion of customer satisfaction dealt with the customer being adequately or inadequately rewarded (Howard & Sheth, 1969). In other words, it was an emotional response to the experiences provided by the customer's association with a software development project (Westbrook & Reilly, 1983). Customer satisfaction was also the outcome of paying for a software development project, whereby the customer compares the results of a project with the expected consequences (Churchill & Surprenant, 1982).

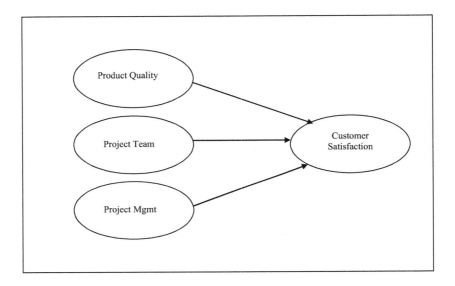

Figure 1. Diagram of the Model

In order to understand the degree of customer satisfaction that exists, it is important to determine the customer requirements for a project using agile-driven or plan-driven software development methods. One way was to collect a series of critical incidents. According to Hayes (1998), a critical incident is a specific example of how software development methods performed in a positive or negative manner. A good critical incident is not only specific, but also describes software development methodology in behavioral terms, using specific adjectives (Hayes, 1998). The idea is that a critical incident describes a single behavior that can be interpreted in the same way by different people.

When examining customer satisfaction for agile-driven and plan-driven software development methodologies, it was important to ask not only whether the customer was satisfied with the results of a software development project, but also if the customer would use the same software development methodology in the future. A second criterion was whether a customer would recommend the software development methodology to a friend, or a business associate. Another criterion was the worth of a software development methodology in terms of quality, cost, and its ability to contribute to the completion of a project in a timely manner compared with the ability of other projects similar in size.

Product Quality

For Hayes (1998), there were two approaches to finding critical incidents - group and individual interviewing. After obtaining the list of critical incidents, the results from the two approaches would be analyzed to find common ground. Next, the customer requirements that were obtained would be used to define the quality of the product. According to Hayes (1998), correctness, reliability, usability, maintainability, testability, portability, inter-operability, intra-operability, and flexibility were the relevant software quality issues. Correctness was the degree to which the software product satisfies customer specifications. Reliability was the extent that software product performed its intended functions (Hayes, 1998). Usability was defined as the effort needed to understand the product resulting from a software development project. Maintainability was the effort required to correct mistakes or errors, whereas testability was the amount of work required to ensure that a software product performs its intended functions (Hayes, 1998). Portability was the process of transferring the software development methods from one project to another project. Inter-operability was the ability to coordinate multiple projects using similar or different software development methods, and intra-operability was the capacity for the components of a software product to communicate with each other (Hayes, 1998). Finally, flexibility was the capability of using a given software development methodology in other projects.

Project Team Effectiveness

Project team effectiveness deals with the human element of a project. It includes the responsiveness of the project team to customer issues, the speed in which customer issues are incorporated into the software product, the availability of the team to focus on customer requirements and issues, the professionalism of the project team, and the enthusiasm of the project team (Kerzner, 2006). These issues were examined in this study because a major assumption of agile-driven methods is that customers actively interact with the project team throughout the course of a project. Customers are not merely bystanders who cheer the project team onward to success, but are considered members of a project team, guiding the team to a successful conclusion (Highsmith, 2004).

Project Management Effectiveness

The last independent variable is project management effectiveness. It is a standard issue in any project, regardless of the methodology employed. According to Kerzner (2006), project management effectiveness can be expressed in terms of the following questions:

1. Did the project finish in the stated timeframe?
2. Was the project planning complete from beginning to end?
3. Did the project manager understand how much time the project required?
4. Was the project completed under, on, or above budget?

In this study, the answers to the above questions were weighed against similar responses from projects that did not use agile-driven methods. If the answers had not been statistically significant when compared with other software development methods, it would have implied that customers were satisfied with the agile-driven methodology employed, but would have been equally satisfied with using plan-driven methods. The key was to verify that not only was the customer satisfied with the use and results of agile-driven software development methods, but also that the customer was satisfied over and above his or her satisfaction level had an organization used a plan-driven software development methodology.

Summary and Conclusion

The significance of the study stemmed from the fact that little empirical research had been conducted in establishing whether customer satisfaction in the use and results of agile-driven software development methods was greater than the customer satisfaction in the use and results of plan-driven software development methods. Most of the literature has been either anecdotal in nature or consisted of a simulation (Cao, 2005; Cao, 2006). Furthermore, there has been no research verifying whether the customer satisfaction in the use and results of plan-driven software development methods is greater than the customer satisfaction in the use and results of agile-driven software development methods. Because it turned out that the use and results of neither software development method yielded customer satisfaction levels greater than the other, the outcome is significant. It indicated that both methods satisfy their respective customers under a wide range of different situations. The research in this study is significant because it helps delineate when and where to employ agile-driven and plan-driven software development methodologies.

CHAPTER 2 – LITERATURE REVIEW

From February 11th to the 13th of 2001, at The Lodge at the Snowboard ski resort in the Wasatch Mountains of Utah, 17 men met to relax, ski, and talk about software development. The group named itself the "Agile Alliance", and after two days of meetings and some fun, these 17 people were surprised to find how much they had in common (Highsmith, 2001). They agreed that the core of their software philosophy was a set of values based on trust and respect, where good products are delivered to customers by individuals who are the most important assets of the companies employing them (Highsmith, 2001). The output of the meeting was entitled a *Manifesto for Agile Software Development*, and was signed by all of the participants. There was one concern voiced by Martin Fowler, a British subject, who felt that most Americans would incorrectly pronounce the word "agile" (Highsmith, 2001).

The *Agile Manifesto* was essentially a statement of values and principles that bears to be repeated. It said:

> We are uncovering better ways of developing software by doing it and helping others doing it. Through this work we have come to value: Individuals and interactions over process and tools, Working software over comprehensive documentation, Customer collaboration over contract negotiation, Responding to change over following a plan. That is, where there is value in the items on the right, we value the items on the left more. (Beck, et al., 2001)

The *Agile Manifesto* continued by stating a set of principles that formed the basis of the agile-driven perspective. The principles are the pillars that support this revolutionary document along with the resulting movement that is currently dominating the software development culture. The principles include:

1. Customer satisfaction is the highest priority and is achieved via the rapid and continuous delivery of useful and valuable software.

2. Changing requirements are welcomed anytime in the software development life cycle, because agile processes harness and promote a customer's competitive advantage.

3. Software delivery occurs frequently, ranging from a few weeks to a couple of months, with the preference towards short timescales.

4. Business people and software developers should work closely together throughout a project.

5. Projects center about motivated individuals who are given the environment, trust, and support needed to do their jobs effectively.

6. The most effective and efficient method of communication between team members is face-to-face conversation.

7. Software that works is the ultimate measure of progress.

8. Agile processes promote and indefinite, sustainable, and a constant rate of software development.

9. Agility is enhanced by good design and continuous attention to technical excellence.

10. Agility embraces simplicity, or the art of maximizing the work not done.

11. In agile projects, the best architectures, requirements, and designs surface from using self-organizing teams.

12. Periodically, agile teams deliberate on becoming more effective, and then proceed to behave accordingly (Beck et al., 2001).

The second through twelfth items in the list are concerned with the operational aspects of developing and managing a software development project. Only the first principle deals with the fundamental goals of the agile movement; namely, to ensure that customer satisfaction is the number one priority in an agile-driven software development project. The key to understanding the first principle is that customer satisfaction must occur early, and remain at nearly the same level over the life of a project (Beck et al., 2001). The second characteristic of the first principle is that there should be an almost continuous delivery of software available for customers to evaluate (Anderson, 2004).

Agile-Driven Methods

Characteristics of Agile-Driven Methods

Boehm and Turner (2004) classified agile-driven methods according to its characteristics, and then proceeded to provide concrete examples of these different techniques. Agile-driven methods were defined as "lightweight processes that employ short iterative cycles; actively involve users to establish, prioritize, and verify requirements; and rely on tacit knowledge within a team as opposed to documentation" (Boehm & Turner, 2004. p. 17). The implication is that for a process to be truly agile, it must be iterative over several cycles, incrementally delivering the product. It must employ self-organizing teams that manage themselves by determining the best way to do the work. Finally, the processes, principles, and work structures must emerge during the course of the project, rather than be pre-determined (Boehm & Turner, 2004).

Agile-driven methods can also be viewed from an operational perspective. Agility embraces change, making it an ally and a friend rather than a hard and cruel taskmaster. Agile-driven methods promote creativity within an agile-driven software development team by delivering exceptionally fast value to the customer (Boehm & Turner, 2004). In an agile-driven project, many releases of a software application are scheduled. The intent is to ensure that only the highest priority functions are implemented first, thereby quickly delivering value to the customer, and promoting the timely emerging of requirements (Boehm & Turner, 2004). The key to employing agile-driven methods is to strip a design to what is just currently being developed with the hidden agenda that change is inevitable, and that planning for future functionality is a waste of time and energy (Boehm & Turner, 2004). Another feature of agility is that a software product may need to be restructured to remove duplication of code, to improve communication among modules and/or subsystems, and to add flexibility without changing the behavior of the application (Boehm & Turner, 2004).

According to Boehm and Turner (2004), when generating the source code of a software application, agile-driven methods can employ paired programming teams, where two programmers worked side by side, collaborating on the same design, algorithms, code, or test procedures. In an empirical study conducted at the University of Utah, Erdogmus (2003) observed that there was a significant economic advantage to paired programmers over solo programmers. However, this is not necessarily a surprising result, because increasing returns to scale is a well-known microeconomic phenomenon that occurs when companies or teams are very small.

Other features of agility include an evaluation of the work performed, the methods employed, and estimates made after an iteration is completed (Boehm & Turner, 2004). The purpose of the action is to encourage teams to learn and reflect upon what happened in the past so that estimates of future activities are more accurate. Thus, tacit knowledge is gained by the project team members rather than being lost or having the information being recorded in a document (Boehm & Turner, 2004). When it would be imperative that written documentation exist, such as in a classified or highly sensitive project, this feature of agility could possess some serious negative implications (Boehm & Turner, 2004).

Types of Agile-Driven Methods

    Extreme Programming. Like most ideas, the agile movement has splintered into a variety of different techniques and methodologies. One of the more famous agile-driven methods is *Extreme Programming* (XP). Beck and Andres (2004), Ambler and Jeffries (2002), and Beck and Fowler (2000), defined extreme programming and discussed its guiding principles, talked about how to model extreme programming projects, and described how to plan extreme programming software projects. Ambler (2002, 2004, and 2006) wrote at length about many of the problems that can appear during an agile-driven software development project using the extreme programming methodology. Jeffries et al. (2000) discussed how to work with on-site customers, how to define requirements with use cases, how to estimate the time and cost of each use case, and how to perform continuous integration and frequent iterations. Thus, it is clear that extreme programming is currently a well-defined set of principles and practices.

    Adaptive Software Development. Highsmith (2000) created an agile-driven method known as *Adaptive Software Development* (ASD), where software teams are exposed to extreme competition in order to deliver products in a timely manner. The intent of the methodology is to support an adaptive software development culture where change and uncertainty are normal, to guide an iterative process using frameworks, to institute collaboration on interpersonal, cultural, and structural levels, and to add rigor and discipline so that the development processes are scalable based upon the uncertainty and complexity of a given project. Greenfield et al. (2004) created a dialect of ASD to reduce the costs of building reusable assets, such as patterns, languages, frameworks, and tools employed to solve specific software problems. Highsmith (2002) discussed the various agile-driven methods, including ASD, by examining a variety of case studies, showing how ASD works in practice.

    Crystal Methods. The *Crystal Method* was developed by Cockburn (2004), where the seven principles include frequent delivery, reflective improvement, osmotic communication, personal safety, focus, easy access to expert users, and a technical environment with automated testing, configuration management, and frequent integration. The point of the agile-driven methodology is to encourage software developers to achieve the above properties rather than follow specific procedures (Cockburn, 2004). The idea is to show that small teams are quite effective at developing software that is fit for the purpose intended by adhering to a few basic development practices, and then by following the proper team dynamics (Cockburn, 2004). In other words, Crystal Methods illustrates why small teams are much more effective and predictable than large teams that follow a bureaucratic and dictatorial process. Cockburn (2004) also identified that Crystal Methods principles apply not only for software development projects, but also for other activities that are results-oriented.

Scrum. *Scrum* is another agile-driven method that was first coined by Takeuchi and Nonaka (1986). Essentially, a "scrum" in rugby occurs when the "players from each team huddle closely together and clash with the players from the opposing team in an attempt to advance down the playing field" (Highsmith, 2002, p. 242). Takeuchi and Nonaka (1986) noted that managers must adopt a more flexible and holistic approach to product development, where development teams work as a single unit to achieve a common goal. Thus, Scrum can be characterized by a built-in instability, self-organizing project teams, overlapping development phases, multi-learning, subtle control, and an organizational transfer of learning.

Schwaber (1996) modified the technique for software development, and attempted to demonstrate that Scrum reduces risk and uncertainty by ensuring that the issues can be transparent early in a software project life cycle, so that appropriate adjustments can be made in a timely manner. Highsmith (2002) observed that Scrum has a distinctive project management flavor where the interaction of team members is predicated upon the belief that communication, collaboration, coordination, and knowledge are critical (Highsmith, 2002). Schwaber (2004) maintained that Scrum yields productivity gains at least an order of magnitude in size by attempting to demonstrate that the software development methodology reduces risk and uncertainty, making them visible early in a software project life cycle.

Feature Driven Development. Coad et al. (1999) advocated using four colors to represent four archetype forms that frequently appear in component and object models. The authors then substituted these archetypes into a 12-class, domain-neutral component, and then applied them to a wide range of business areas. In the process, the agile-driven methodology known as *Feature Driven Development* (FDD) was created, where modeling and development are optimized via a minimalist, five-step process, and where tangible and working results are delivered on time and within budget. The key is that the stereotypes known as role, moment-interval party, place or thing, and description appear repeatedly in component models. By employing color, FDD attempts to ensure that the overall shape of the model is accurately portrayed.

Dynamic Systems Development. According to Highsmith (2002), the *Dynamic Systems Development Model* (DSDM) was developed in the United Kingdom during the 1990s, and was an outgrowth of existing rapid application development (RAD) processes. The principles of DSDM include active user involvement, frequent delivery, team decision making, integrated testing throughout the course of the software project life cycle, and reversible changes in development (Highsmith, 2002). There are three phases of the DSDM development process, including the functional model iteration, the design and build iteration, and the implementation iteration.

The functional model iteration consists of gathering and then prototyping the functional requirements originating from an initial list of prioritized requirements (Highsmith, 2002). The design and build iteration hones the prototype so that it meets the specified functional and non-functional requirements (Highsmith, 2002). The implementation iteration places the software application in the user's environment. Although Highsmith (2002) gave the initial impression that the three iterative cycles are distinct, the author also stated that there is usually considerable overlap in the functional iteration, design and build iteration, and the implementation iteration.

Lean Development. Finally, *Lean Development* (LD) is the least known of the various agile-driven methods. Charette (2002) seemed to have first created this proprietary methodology, deriving it from the principles of lean production. According to Highsmith (2002), it embodies the notion of "dynamic instability" that is similar to Scrum's concept of "controlled chaos" or the Adaptive Software Development idea of "balancing on the edge of chaos". Charette (2002) and Poppendieck and Poppendieck (2006) derived and expanded on lean development's twelve principles, where customer satisfaction is given the highest priority. The focus of lean development is to create rapidly visible customer value, build change tolerant software, generate only the necessary functionality, and aggressiveness, stubbornness, and belief in meeting the goals of the methodology (Highsmith, 2002). As a short aside, Highsmith (2002) observed that Charette believed the baseline to measuring improvement is a level three organization adhering to the Software Engineering Institute's (SEI) Capability Maturity Model (CMM). This is noteworthy because CMM is clearly a plan-driven software development methodology.

Conclusion

Thus, what is readily apparent is that the various agile-driven methodologies that emerged out of the fateful two days in February of 2001 appear to be different manifestations of the same idea – agility. The fundamental ideas of the different techniques are high customer satisfaction, rapid software development, and highly qualified software developers and engineers interacting effectively with the other members of cross-functional teams.

Plan-Driven Methods

Characteristics of Plan-Driven Methods

According to Boehm and Turner (2004), plan-driven methods are generally thought to be traditional ways to develop software. The methods approach software development from the perspective of mainline engineering fields, where the requirements/design/build paradigm promotes orderly processes focus on continuous improvement (Boehm & Turner, 2004). The general idea behind a plan-driven approach is based on the tenets of systems engineering, where a large number of components are produced by a single company employing a cadre of workers. The advantage of a plan-driven strategy is that it works well when developing hardware components, but software development may be a horse of a different color. Software has logical constraints rather than physical constraints (Boehm & Turner, 2004). The result of this dichotomy is that software projects are typically late, over budget, and of poor to mediocre product quality. In response, the Department of Defense developed a series of documents to help software developers create applications for the defense establishment, including MIL-STD-1521, DoD-STD-2167, and MIL-STD- 498 and their successors (Boehm & Turner, 2004). In the private sector, companies such as IBM, Hitachi, and Siemens also developed similar standards (Boehm & Turner, 2004).

Because plan-driven methods are characterized by a systematic approach to software development, the software application usually moves through a series of well-defined steps from requirements to finished executable code. Thus, it becomes paramount that the documentation thoroughly authenticates the workings of a software application, regardless of whether the development cycle follows a waterfall model or is rather incremental or evolutionary in nature (Highsmith, 2004). One of the problems with plan-driven methods is that software developers view documentation as an anathema, sometimes openly rebelling against the need for meticulous documentation, and at other times, carelessly and insidiously ignoring the necessity for accurate and precise records.

Because software is malleable, plan-driven software development methods scrupulously define, standardize, and incrementally improve software processes, detailed plans, activities, workflows, roles and responsibilities, and work product descriptions (Highsmith, 2004). The implication is that individuals are trained to monitor, control, and educate the infrastructure (Highsmith, 2004). The advantages of plan-driven methods are derived from the Industrial Revolution, where specific processes were repeated, specific work performed, and where any individual could examine and understand the work accomplished.

Thus plan-driven software development methods allow individuals to move from project to project without a significant amount of retraining, where the loss of a key contributor does not adversely affect the success of a project.

One of the key concepts of plan-driven software development methods includes *process improvement*, where a group of activities are designed to improve the performance and maturity of an organization's processes (Highsmith, 2004). Another key notion is that of *process capability* or the "inherent ability of a process to produce planned results" (Highsmith, 2004, p. 12). In other words, as a process improves, it becomes more measurable and predictable so that product quality is enhanced and productivity is assured. Furthermore, as would be expected, organizations mature in the sense that processes become standardized across the great divide that sometimes separates functional departments, ensuring that common assets are effectively deployed. Specialists congregate together to ensure the integrity of the processes employed, and to measure and assess the uncertainties that can result in a significant loss or harm to the firm (Highsmith, 2004). *Verification* confirms that specifications, designs, and models reflect the specified requirements, whereas *validation* is employed to determine the fitness of a product to its mission (Highsmith, 2004). Finally, to achieve these characteristics, a software system architecture is created to identify the software and system components, connectors, and constraints; to understand the needs of the system stakeholders; and to show how the system components, connectors, and constrains actually satisfy the needs of the system stakeholders (Highsmith, 2004).

It should not be forgotten that strict planning can impede innovation, and thus become the object of stifling asphyxiation. The danger of plan-driven software development methods is that its team members can become like mechanical androids being so focused on the process that he or she loses sight of the big picture (Highsmith, 2004). On the other hand, plan-driven methods that have managerial support, organizational infrastructure, and seasoned practitioners can thwart the onslaught of an unnecessary concentration of effort. Some of the advantages of plan-driven software development methods include the existence of component libraries that encourage software reuse, and a well-trained staff that understand the value of creating and maintaining effective documentation (Highsmith, 2004).

Types of Plan-Driven Methods

Military Standards. Like agile-driven software development methods, plan-driven software development methods have diverged into an assortment of distinctive techniques and methodologies. In the beginning, military standards were all the rage. DoD-STD-2167 possessed a document-driven line of attack for data item descriptions and deliverables, even though the standard encompassed the complete software development life cycle (Highsmith, 2004). MIL-STD-1521 describes how to conduct sequential reviews and audits. MIL-STD-498 revised DoD-STD-2167 by giving additional flexibility for systems engineering, as well as software planning and development. The key to military software development standards is to state specifically how software is developed, thereby making the discipline more like civil, mechanical, and electrical engineering practices (Boehm & Turner, 2004).

ISO, EIA, and IEEE Standards. The Institute of Electrical and Electronics Engineers (IEEE) generalized MIL-STD-498 by creating EIA/IEEE J-STD-016 to encompass commercial software processes (Highsmith, 2004). According to Gray (1999), there are only cosmetic differences between the two standards, because for each detailed requirement in MIL-STD-498 there is a corresponding requirement in J-STD-016-1995 with the same technical content. Furthermore, two additional activities in J-STD-016 that deal with updating systems and software requirements that were needed for software that is built as is. There is an additional traceability requirement that is similar to the traceability requirements in MIL-STD-498 (Gray, 1999). Every other feature in J-STD-016 was also contained in MIL-STD-498.

As plan-driven software development methodologies have progressed, J-STD-016 evolved into ISO/IEC 12207 and IEEE/EIA 12207. Most of the topics included in J-STD-016 are also covered by the corresponding ISO and IEEE standards, namely ISO 12207 and ISO 15504 (Gray, 1999). The ISO 9000 standard has experienced two renderings, first the 1994 standard followed by the 2000 standard. The 1994 standard consists of three conformance standards (i.e., ISO 9001, 9002, and 9003), and two guidance standards (i.e., ISO 9000-1 and ISO 9004-1), where the more inclusive standard possessed the lower number (Peach, 1997). Essentially, ISO 9000/1994 is made up of 20 specific quality assurance requirements, ranging from management responsibility, to process control to finally statistical techniques (Peach, 1997). In contrast, ISO 9000/2000 is a process management and improvement methodology that establishes the responsibilities for managing a process, defines the process, identifies customer requirements, establishes measures for process performance, compares process performance with customer requirements, identifies process improvement opportunities, and improves the actual process performance (Hooper, 2002).

Software Factories. The software factory method is a long-range and integrated software development methodology designed to enhance software quality, software reuse, and software development productivity (Boehm & Turner, 2004). According to Cusumano

(1989), Bemer (1968) proposed that General Electric develop a software factory to reduce the variance in programmer productivity by employing standardized tools with a computer-based interface along with a historical database of financial and management controls. In contrast, McIlroy (1968) emphasized the ability systematically to reuse source code when creating new computer programs. Although there was some resistance to the employment of standardized tools and reusable software, the ideas became entrenched into the discipline of software engineering (Boehm & Turner, 2004).

Cusumano (1988) outlined the Japanese concern for reusability, given that as of 1986, approximately 94% of all software products sold in Japan were completely or partially customized, or designed for integrated software systems. Hitachi, Toshiba, NEC, and Fujitsu incrementally introduced standardized software processes with an emphasis on process and quality control (Cusumano, 1988). The apparent reason for establishing software factories was to develop automated tools, design support, program generation, test support, reuse support, and project management support to gain a competitive advantage by providing software products that would be superior in performance to software substitutes, but lower in price (Cusumano, 1988). In contrast, Piore and Sabel (1984) observed that mass production is in general obsolete, because customers demand more variety in the products that he or she purchases, and workers desire discretion in the work environment. Accordingly, flexible specialization that uses a number of small but specialized suppliers that employ skilled workers was supplementing mass production in large organizations (Piore & Sable, 1984).

Aaen et al. (1997) evaluated contrasting views on software factories by discussing the various strengths and weaknesses of the Japanese, European, and North American approaches to the subject. The Japanese approached the subject from an industrialized software organization, the Europeans from a generic perspective, and the North Americans from an experience-based or a mature-based viewpoint (Aaen et al., 1997). To understand the various software factory approaches, it is necessary to know their context, objective, strategy, organization, and implementation.

Under the Japanese approach, the software factory methodology is employed when the context is developing control systems, the objective is to increase software quality, and the strategy is to develop, support, and manage the software development process (Aaen et al., 1997). Furthermore, the organization is concerned with work benchmarks, project management, reusability, measuring productivity, measuring quality, and quality circles; and the implementation is comprehensive (Aaen et al., 1997). Under the European perspective, the context consists of large companies, computer manufacturers, software house, research institution, and universities, and the objective is to generate an integrated software development environment where the goal is to adapt a factory environment to an organization rather than vice versa (Aaen et al., 1997). The strategy is to ensure the software components adhere to prescribed standards allowing them to communicate with one another, the organizations is made up of users in work context environments that promote the work of software developers (Aaen et al., 1997). Finally, the implementation of improvement is bent on establishing technological infrastructures tailored to fit with product and process issues, such as systematic reusability, computer-aided tools, integration, etc. (Aaen et al., 1997).

In an experience-based software factory, the context is the Software Engineering Laboratory, a consortium between the NASA/Goddard Space Flight Center and the Computer Science Corporation (Aaen et al., 1997). The objective is to increase the effectiveness of the software process, reduce the level or rework, and reuse life-cycle products. The strategy is continuous improvement employing the plan, execute, analyze, and synthesize the model (Aaen et al., 1997). The organization is project oriented where the focus is on problem solving, and the implementation of improvement requiring an incremental management approach (Aaen et al., 1997). On the other hand, in a mature software organization, the context is the Capability Maturity Model (CMM) where the five levels of software quality include the initial, repeatable, defined, managed and optimizing stages. The objective is to provide a software improvement methodology that promotes predictable, reliable, and self-improving software development processes that ensure the creation of high-quality software (Aaen et al., 1997). The strategy of CMM is to perform step-wise improvements in organizing software, where each maturity level consists of key processes and practices (Paulk et al., 1994). The organization of the software is done in a disciplined manner where the planning and tracking is stable, and based on previous successes. The key to managing an implementation is to employ the continuous improvement process where top management are committed to the methodology, resistance to improvements are identified, allowing the individuals closest to the processes to improve them (Aaen et al., 1997).

Cleanroom Methodology. Mills et al. (1987) developed the cleanroom software development methodology. Although the name was derived from the electronics industry, where physical clean rooms exists to minimize the introduction of defects when fabricating hardware, the cleanroom methodology is a theory-based, team oriented process approach, ensuring that high quality software is generated in an economical manner (Prowell et al., 1999). The purpose of cleanroom software development methodology is to combine the formal methods of object-based box structure specification and design, function-theoretic correctness verification, and statistical process control to develop software with minimal or zero defects (Hausler et al. 1994). One of the purported benefits of cleanroom software development is that a known and certified mean time to failure can be measured (Dyer, 1992). The approach merges mathematical-based methods of specification, design, and correctness verification, and statistical, usage-based testing to ensure that the software developed is fit to use (Ananthpadmanabhan et al., n.d.). Cleanroom software development methodology is predicated on a set of formal specifications that employ a stepwise refinement and verification process that starts from a black box model. Over time, the state boxes that represent the external behavior of the software plus the data required to implement the behavior evolve in a state-wise manner into a clear box, where the behavior, the data, and the procedures needed to implement that behavior become transparent (Ananthpadmanabhan et al., n.d.).

The purported benefits of the cleanroom software development methodology is that it purports to increase the amount of errors discovered early during the testing phase of the software development life cycle, which in turn may leads to longer product life, shorter development times, and lower overall costs (Linger & Trammel, 1996). For each iteration, the cleanroom methodology employs statistical quality control in the software development lifecycle, thereby ensuring that each iteration is in statistical control using pre-defined standards. In other words, software testing is perceived as a statistical experiment, where a representative sample of all possible software uses are randomly generated, and the performance of the sample can be used to draw conclusions about the overall operation of the software application (Linger & Trammel, 1996). The economic benefits arise from the technical benefits, where there are few failures experienced in the field, reductions in cycle time, and ease of maintenance due to a longer product life (Mills et al., 1987).

Capability Maturity Model. According to Paulk et al. (1994), in November of 1986 the Software Engineering Institute (SEI) along with the MITRE Corporation developed a maturity framework that would permit both organizations to improve their software processes. The intent was to select qualified software contractors. Over a half a year later, the Humphrey (1987) wrote a brief description of a software process maturity framework. In a later work, Humphrey (1989) expanded the thesis, generating a software process assessment that appraises an organization's current software processes, and a software capability evaluation that identifies qualified individuals to develop software or monitor a software process. Four years later, Paulk et al. (1991) and Weber et al. (1991) developed the Capability Maturity Model for software development.

The CMM is based on knowledge that is acquired from actual software process assessments, as well as from feedback from industry and government. The model is organized into five levels, each of which is a plateau of increasing maturity (Humphrey, 1994). The initial level is the first state. It is characterized by ad hoc and sometimes chaotic processes where success depends on the valiant efforts and heroics of specific individuals. The second level is the repeatable level, where the project management processes focuses on cost, schedule, and functionality (Humphrey, 1994). The third level is the defined level, where both the management and software engineering activities are documented, standardized, and integrated into a firm's software processes (Humphrey, 1994). The fourth level is the managed level, where detailed data regarding a company's software processes and product quality are collected and analyzed quantitatively. The last or fifth level is the optimizing level, which occurs when continuous improvement is facilitated via quantitative feedback from the software process, and by leading change through the use of innovative technologies (Humphrey, 1994).

Paulk et al. (1994) stated that CMM is an application of the process management concepts inherent in Total Quality Management (TQM). Customer satisfaction is the goal of CMM, even though it is not explicitly stated that a customer should be satisfied with a software product (Paulk et al., 1994). Although Paulk et al. (1994) acknowledged that CMM should be more proactive in addressing customer satisfaction; the authors categorically stated that customer satisfaction is a critical component of an organization's process improvements or quality management efforts. Although CMM deals with the processes of a software supplier, CMM does not directly discuss the customer-supplier relationship. Even so, the customer is integral to the software processes, and shares in the responsibility in providing for the software development environment (Humphrey, 1994). The advantage of CMM is that it was a collection of processes and practices that were developed by a broad spectrum of practitioners. The opinions of hundreds of software developers were solicited, and although there was not unanimous agreement on conflicting recommendations, CMM appears to represent the consensus of a large number of software engineers (Humphrey, 1994).

Capability Maturity Model Integration. The Capability Maturity Model Integration (CMMI) is a successor of CMM, and was developed between from 1987 to 1997 by industry, government, and the SEI, where v1.2 was released in August, 2006 (Chrissis et al., 2006). The three versions of the model include CMMI Development, CMMI Services, and CMMI Acquisitions. Currently, CMMI Development consists of 22 processes areas, including causal analysis and resolution, measurement and analysis, process and product quality assurance, and validation and verification (Chrissis et al., 2006). Each process possesses between one to four goals, where each goal is comprised of a number of practices. Some of the goals and practices are specific to a given process area, whereas other goals and practices are of a generic nature. The three different classes of appraisals are classes A, B, and C, where an appraisal team is required for class A and was quite formal, but it was optional for classes B and C. The results of an appraisal for class A is published on the SEI website (i.e., http://www.sei.org), and is the only appraisal form that can result in an actual rating (Chrissis et al. 2006).

There are two different versions of CMMI, one being staged where group processes are broken up into five maturity levels, which have evolved from the five levels of the CMM. These levels include the initial level, the managed level, the defined level, the quantitatively managed level, and the optimizing level (Kulpa, 2003). The continuous version of CMMI is very similar to the original CMM, but with defined capability within a given profile (Chrissis et al., 2006). The differences between the continuous version of CMMI and CMM are mostly organizational, where the content is the same.

Turner and Jain (2002) attempted to combine CMMI and agile-driven methods, pointing out that the two approaches have quite a bit in common. According to these authors, there is no "right" way to develop software, but for different phases in a project, one methodology is better than the other (Turner & Jain, 2002). One such combination would be the marrying of project management and earned value management (Solomon, 2002). Similar nuptials were discussed by Nawrocki et al. (2002), where extreme programming techniques would be evaluated by the CMMI methodology. For example, it was determined that the XP requirements management approach where oral communication was preferred over written communication, but is not compliant with CMMI (Nawrocki et al., 2002).

Personal Software Process and Team Software Process. The last of the plan-driven methods are the Personal Software Process (PSP) and the Team Software Process (TSP), both developed by Humphrey (1994, 1996, and 1999). According to Boehm and Turner (2004), PSP is a structured outline of form, guidelines, and procedures for measuring and improving an individual's programming skills. TSP expands the features of PSP to ensure the development of industrial-strength software by employing team planning and control techniques.

Humphrey (1994) observed that the Personal Software Process is a self-improvement process that has a maturity framework, much like the Capability Maturity Model. PSP0 is the baseline process that includes basic measurements and reporting (Humphrey, 1994).

Essentially, PSP0 is the current process employed to write software, but enhanced by incorporating measurements. PSP0.1 augments PSP0 by including a coding standard, size measurements, and the *process improvement proposal* (PIP), a form that records process problems, experiences, and improvement suggestions (Humphrey, 1994). PSP1 adds a test report along with a size and resource estimation (Humphrey, 1994). PSP1.1 introduces schedule and task planning. PSP2 increases the reporting by adding review techniques to help find defects early on in the software development life cycle (Humphrey, 1996). The purpose of PSP2.1 is to establish design completeness criteria by examining different design verification and consistency techniques. Finally, PSP3 is a cyclical process that is used in testing incrementally a software program by considering the quality of the current increment and ignoring the quality of previous increments (Humphrey, 1996). If the current increment caused problems with previous increments, then earlier tests are rerun using the technique known as *regression testing*.

The Team Software Process is a software development methodology that emphasizes planning, measurements, scripts, and accountability with the end-result being high quality source code (Humphrey, 1999). The idea is to model the development of software development from the perspective of a team using the life cycle approach as a framework. According to Humphrey (1999), most programming students do not have a significant amount of experience working in teams. The implication is that the purpose of TSP is to provide a model for team software development that allows programmers to generate quality software in a timely manner.

Conclusion

Similar to the agile-driven methodologies previously examined, there have been a number of plan-driven methodologies developed. What is evident from this literature review is that the plan-driven methodologies are an attempt to bring structure and engineering formalism to software development. It is reminiscent of Taylor's (1911) treatise on scientific management, where efficient production methods were substituted for work gangs. George and Jones (1996) aptly pointed out that scientific management attempted to simplify a job by encouraging specialization, but the problem with the methodology was that workers lost control over their work behaviors. The result was a loss in productivity. If the analogy is correct, it would have turned out that the use and results of agile-driven software development methods increased customer satisfaction over and above the use and results of plan-driven software development methods.

Literature Review of the Model Variables

Agile-driven software development methods are in its infancy, and not much is known about how the use and results of the method actually satisfies customers. Anderson (2004) observed that because of the recent outsourcing of jobs, "management techniques must improve and working practices must change to deliver more value, more often, in order to improve competitiveness", suggesting a need for methods to produce better results, and, thus, happier customers (p. xxvi). Highsmith (2004) wrote that the core values of agile-driven methods consists of valuing individuals and interactions over processes and tools, working products over extensive documentation, customer collaboration over contract negotiations, and responding to changes over merely following a plan. Boehm and Turner (2004) believed that agile-driven methods were lightweight processes, employing short iterative cycles and actively involving the users in the development of products. Thus, by adding more value to a project, it follows that the use and results of agile-driven software development methods supposedly satisfy customers more than the use and results of plan-driven software development methods. Hence, the purpose of this dissertation is to discover if the use and results of agile-driven software development methods do indeed significantly enhance customer satisfaction more than the use and results of plan-driven software development methods.

Construct Elements

The construct elements are customer satisfaction, product quality, project team effectiveness and project management effectiveness. Each one of the variables has undergone extensive scrutiny in the literature, but because agile-driven methods have only recently appeared on the scene, no one has actually shown empirically whether these independent variables actually contribute to satisfying the customer in an agile-driven software development setting (Beck et al., 2001). The purpose of this section is to review briefly the literature on each one of the variables.

Customer Satisfaction. As a process, customers and even stakeholders can evaluate an experience by deciding whether a project was as good as it was promoted (Hunt, 1977). Customers can also evaluate a project in terms of the available alternatives and determine if a project was consistent with a customer's prior beliefs (Engle & Blackwell, 1982). Customer satisfaction can be viewed as the difference between prior expectations and the actual performance after the project was completed (Tse & Wilton, 1988). Essentially, the maximization of customer satisfaction is a win-win situation with far-reaching impacts (Vavra, 1997).

Measuring customer satisfaction has had a long-standing history and is one of the goals of Total Quality Management (Kan, 1995). The advantage of monitoring customer satisfaction of agile-driven software development methods is that it can provide detailed information about the technique. According to the pronouncements from the agile-driven community, customer satisfaction using agile-driven methods seems to be almost a non sequitur (Highsmith, 2004). The fact that the methodology demands that customers become intimately involved in an agile-driven software development project seems to indicate that he or she would necessarily be satisfied with the final product. Thus, it is apparent that this conclusion needs to be confirmed empirically by examining data that indicate whether the pronouncements are justified.

Table 1 *Product Quality Definitions and Dimensions*

Quality Definitions	Quality Dimensions
Correctness	The degree that the project methods met customer specifications.
Reliability	The extent that project methods performed its intended functions.
Usability	The effort required to understand the results of the project.
Maintainability	The effort required to find and correct errors.
Testability	The effort required to ensure that the project performed its intended functions.
Portability	The effort needed to transfer the project methods from one project to another.
Inter-operability	The effort required to coordinate multiple project using similar or different methods.
Intra-operability	The effort required for the project components to communicate with one another.
Flexibility	The effort required to use the project methods in other projects.

Note: From *Measuring customer satisfaction: Survey design, use, and statistical analysis methods* (2nd ed.), by B. E. Hayes, 1998, Milwaukee, WI: American Society for Quality. p. 15. Copyright 1998 by B. E. Hayes. Adopted with permission.

Product Quality. Quality is something that needs no introduction. McCall (1979) was apparently the first to discuss the characteristics of quality software, and the characteristics are included in the quality dimensions that appear in Table 1. These quality features tend to promote progress, stability, compliance and a certain amount of quality effort (MacMillan & Vosburgh, 1986). The dimensions have practical implications, particularly when attempting to measure the effectiveness of a project.

Typically, the quality for an individual activity is calculated by dividing the number of faults found in the activity by the sum of the number of faults found in the activity plus the number of faults found in other activities (Schulmeyer, 1999). The metric is quite useful when a project is in process and when detailed data are available, but may not be forthcoming at the end of a project or after it is completed. From a customer's standpoint, the quality of a project appears to be an assessment of the whole product, not merely the sum of the quality of the final product's component parts (Murine, 1988).

Project Team Effectiveness. The literature is replete with discussion on cross-functional teams. Scholtes (1988) discussed team development in detail, praising the effectiveness of cross-functional teams. Senge et al. (1994) also advocated cross-functional teams, pointing out the apparent advantages over other organizational forms because it is easy for cross-functional teams to coalesce. In other words, the team encouraged synergy by changing the leadership style from autocratic to participative in nature (Kouzes & Posner, 1987).

Cross-functional teams are the basis of project team effectiveness when employing agile-driven methods (Anderson, 2004). According to Baheti et al. (2002), as well as Erdogmus (2003), when agile-driven software development methods are employed, paired-programmer teams are typical, whereby it was suggested that two programmers work in unison to increase the effectiveness of the programming effort. The idea behind paired-programming teams is to take advantage of economies of scale, where a team of two people can outperform two individuals working separately.

With regard to the research, data about a software development project were collected after the project was completed. The study focused on the perceived effectiveness of the project team from the perspective of the customer and other stakeholders upon completion of the project using a post-test methodology. The effect was a one-time measurement of project team effectiveness at the end of a project, rather than multiple measurements over time.

Project Management Effectiveness. Project management effectiveness essentially revolves around whether a project is completed at an acceptable level of quality, at an expected cost, and is finished in a set timeframe (Kerzner, 2006). Projects are temporary organizations that engage in planned activities, and are constrained by limited resources (Kertzner, 2001). The advantages of the project form of organization is that it permits a manager to respond to clients and the environment, to identify and correct problems, to make timely decisions about conflicting project goals, and to optimize total project performance, rather than the performance of individual tasks (Meredith & Mantel, 2003).

Because the purpose of a project is to achieve a specified objective in a limited amount of time, it makes sense to evaluate a project when it is completed. Rising and Derby (2003), as well as Chin (2004), felt that by incorporating a retrospective analysis at the end of an iteration, team members are better equipped to see a project in its totality, thus ensuring that these individuals work together effectively.

According to the Project Management Institute, there are five major and overlapping processes in a project, including the initiation processes, the planning processes, the executing processes, the controlling processes, and the closing processes (PMBOK Guide, 2005). The initiation processes authorize the project, whereas planning processes defined and refined the project's objectives and goals. The executing processes coordinate the people and the resources. The controlling processes ensure that the objectives and goals are being met, and the closing processes formalize the acceptance of the result by bringing the project to completion (Gray & Larson, 2006). At the end of each process, a certain amount of introspection is necessary to assure that a given process is successful. The analysis is concerned with the quality of the output of the process, the cost of the process, and the timeliness of the process (Gray & Larson, 2006). Thus, to understand the effectiveness of the project management, it makes sense to address the issues at the end of a project. The hidden assumption is that by examining a project after it was completed, the effects are valid for the entire project, whether those effects deal with customer satisfaction, product quality, project team effectiveness, or project management effectiveness.

CHAPTER 3 - METHODOLOGY

Overview

In this chapter, the problem of whether agile-driven software development methods satisfy the customer over and above plan-driven project management methods is restated. The research questions and/or the hypotheses are listed again. A short description of the research design is outlined, and operational definitions of customer satisfaction, product quality, project team effectiveness, and project management effectiveness are provided. The instrument that was developed to capture the values of these operational variables is also described. How projects, companies, and individual customers were selected is discussed. The procedures involved in collecting the data are portrayed, particularly how the SurveyGold software application was employed in collecting responses. The actual data collection method is then described. The methodological assumptions, limitations, and delimitations are then depicted and illustrated, including a discussion of confounding, reliability, and validity. Finally, the relevant ethical assurances are explained, including respect for persons and their autonomy, informed consent, beneficence and non-malfeasance, justice, trust, fidelity to science, and the resolution of ethical conflicts and dilemmas.

Restatement of the Problem

As stated previously, this study examined if the use and results of an agile-driven software development projects satisfied customers more than the use and the results of plan-driven software development projects. The idea of the research was to discover if there was a statistically significant difference in customer satisfaction when a project manager employed agile-driven software development methods rather than plan-driven software development methods. A statistical examination was needed because the proponents of both technologies have claimed that the use and results of each software development methodology significantly satisfies its customers.

Statement of Research Questions and Hypotheses

The research examined and tested the following hypotheses:

H0:   The autonomous customer satisfaction for a project using agile-driven software development methods is equal to the autonomous customer satisfaction for a project using plan-driven software development methods.

H1$_a$: The autonomous customer satisfaction for a project using agile-driven software development methods is greater than the autonomous customer satisfaction for a project using plan-driven software development methods.

H1$_b$: The autonomous customer satisfaction for a project using plan-driven software development methods is greater than the autonomous customer satisfaction for a project using agile-driven software development methods.

The focus was to test whether H0 and H1$_b$ could be rejected at the 95% or 99% levels of confidence. If so, it would mean that the customer satisfaction for projects using agile-driven software development methods was significantly greater than the customer satisfaction for projects using plan-driven software development methods.

The fact that H1$_b$ was included in the hypotheses to be tested is worth discussing. It could have turned out that the use and results of plan-driven software development methods provide greater customer satisfaction than the use and results of agile-driven software development methods. In such case, the characteristics of the data would have required further scrutiny, for under certain conditions or project sizes, plan-driven software development methods may have been the preferred methodology to employ, whereas under other situations agile-driven software development technologies could have been the favored tactic to use. If so, then the statistical evidence would tend to confirm that agile-driven methods have a limited application (Boehm & Turner, 2004).

As was discussed in the previous chapter, product quality, project team effectiveness and project management effectiveness are the three variables that seem to affect customer satisfaction. The intent of the research was to establish a statistical relationship between customer satisfaction, the dependent variable, and product quality, project team effectiveness, and project management effectiveness, the independent variables.

Description of the Research Design

Methodology Discussion

A project is an activity that occurs over a specified period of time, and has a distinct beginning and end (Kerzner, 2006). The time period can be rather short or last for several years. The projects contained in the data were expected to be representative of a wide range of software development projects so that a modicum of generalization could be made, or to put it technically, the research would suffer from a minimum of external threats. Because a software development project contains a plethora of attributes, the time lapse from the beginning of a project to its end may have some bearing on customer satisfaction. Under ideal circumstances, a measure of customer satisfaction could be obtained at the beginning of the project, or pre-test, at periodic time intervals, and at the end of the project, or post-test (Trochim, 2001). By conducting such tests, one could determine whether agile-driven software development methods satisfy the customer throughout the software development life cycle. If there were to be changes in customer satisfaction, a pre-test/post-test methodology would reveal the extent of the change.

According to Cozby (2004), the problem with pre-testing is that it limits the ability to generalize to populations that did not take the pre-test because in the real world individuals are rarely given a pre-test. In contrast, a post-test is a measurement or observation that occurs at the end of an experiment (Cozby, 2004). A post-test observes the effects of the programs or treatments on the study group and is an integral part of any experiment (Trochim, 2001). With a post-test, it is possible to see if the use and results of employing agile-driven software development methods were effective because a post-test occurs after a project is completed.

Actual Research Design

There are numerous problems with a pre-test/post-test research strategy. First, there is the problem of collecting data. Organizations would have had to have been found that were willing to permit the collection of data at specified intervals during the software project life cycle. This in itself is no mean feat, because it is apparent that by periodically measuring the same set of variables, some familiarity with the instrument by the customers and other stakeholders could have biased the results (Trochim, 2001). Respondents could have answered the questions by rote, rather than providing meaningful data. The third issue is concerned with the amount of time expended by the project. It is very possible that the projects being studied could have lasted a year or more, thus unnecessarily delaying the collection of the data and the writing of the dissertation. All of these negative consequences precluded the use of pre-test/post-test methodology in this study. Thus, a post-test only methodology was employed where a participant was asked about a variety of questions about a given software development project after the project was completed.

Operational Definitions of the Variables

An operational definition shows a variable, term, or object in terms of specific processes or validation tests that determine its existence and quantity. According to Deming (1982), an operational definition puts meaning into an idea by characterizing a variable, term, or object in specific terms to ensure that any validation testing is repeatable. Deming (1982) observed that a characteristic, state, or condition does not possess a true value that can be defined in terms of a measurement or an observation. In other words, if there was a change of how a measure is conducted, there would be a change in an operational definition, and an observation would emit a new number (Deming, 1982).

In this research, the dependent variable was customer satisfaction, and the independent variables were product quality, project team effectiveness, and project management effectiveness. Each one of the variables were defined operationally by employing a variety of questions, where each one of the questions used a 5-point Likert-type scale. During the course of responding to the internet survey, a participant was requested to provide an impression of what he or she experienced for each question asked. The use of a 5-point Likert-type scale was an attempt to quantify an individual's familiarity with the software development project being measured.

Because problems occur in every project, it was conceivable that not all of the relevant data were captured by the operational definitions of the four variables listed above. For example, the project team may have lacked knowledge about a firm's products or services, the project team may not have been able to recommend the best way to meet a customer's needs, or the project team did not perform the tasks requested by a customer.

The two types of demographic data that were collected were information about a project and personal information about a given research participant. The project information was concerned with the size of the project in terms of the person hours expended, the number of project team members, and the project's budget. This data were rather useful because under certain conditions the use and results of plan-driven software development projects may have satisfied the customer more than the use and results of agile-driven software development projects. Some of the limitations of the two techniques were achieved by capturing project demographics. Furthermore, demographic data on the research participants were used to shed light on the relative satisfaction levels. For example, an innovator or a solution giver may have been quite satisfied with the use of a certain methodology and the output of the project, but a formal leader, defender, or resister may have only had a modicum of confidence in the results.

Description of the Instrument

Questionnaire Instructions

The instructions were the first section of the questionnaire. It stated that the purpose of the survey was to collect customer satisfaction data regarding the results of using an agile-driven or a plan-driven software development methodology in a project. It also said that the questionnaire consisted of 51 questions, all responses would be anonymous, and all data would be held in confidence. The instructions asserted that it was not possible to identify specific individuals or companies, the data collected would be used in a doctoral dissertation, and the results could appear in an academic or trade publication. The instructions pointed out that if a participant pressed the *Continue* button, then he or she was initially agreeing to participate in the survey. The instructions also observed that if at the end of the questionnaire a participant pressed the *Submit Your Response* button, then he or she was indeed agreeing to include his or her data into the study. Finally, the instructions pointed out that if a participant closed the survey window at any time prior to pressing the *Submit Your Responses* button, his or her data would not be collected.

Project Information

The section introduced a customer to the survey. Its intent was to gather not only the name of the project and the type of project management technique employed but also the data about the project, such as the number of person hours expended, the number of individuals on the project team, the budget, how long ago the project was completed, and both the estimated and actual project duration. The study recognized that not every respondent was privy to all of the data about a project, nor would he or she want to disclose specific information. Thus, a 5-point Likert-type scale was used to capture the information so that the constructs could be estimated without divulging any specific confidential information.

The second question in the survey was particularly important because it asked a participant if the project under consideration was agile-driven, plan-driven, or if the participant knew what software development methodology was employed. If a participant selected the first option, then the questionnaire asked a participant to identify the specific agile-driven methodology used. The option were: (a) Extreme Programming, (b) Adaptive Software Development, (c) Crystal Methods, (d) Scrum, (e) Feature Driven Development, (f) Dynamic Systems Development, (g) Lean Development, (h) Other method, or (i) Did not know the specific agile-driven method used. If a participant selected the second option, then the questionnaire asked a participant to select the specific plan-driven methodology used. The options were: (a) Military Standards, (b) ISO Standard, (c) EIA Standard, (d) IEEE Standard, (e) Software Factory, (f) Cleanroom Methodology, (g) Capability Maturity Model, (h) Capability Maturity Model Integration, (i) Personal Software Process, (j) Team Software Process, (k) Other method, or (l) Did not know the specific plan-driven method used.

In the second question, if a participant chose the third option, then that individual did not know at all what type of software development methodology was used. In this case, a series of three additional questions were asked in order to ascertain what software development methodology was probably employed. The first question attempted to characterize the project based on the whether the project created rapid value and the project members responded quickly, or if the project could be characterized by predictability, stability and a high assurance to anchor project processes. The second question dealt with the environment of the project, where a participant was asked if the project was characterized as turbulent with risks, or whether the requirements were largely determined, making the project relatively stable. The third question discussed the management of the project, where there was a dependence on a dedicated customer representation, or whether there was a dependence on some form of contract between the project team and the customers. If the majority of the responses indicated that the project possessed agile-driven characteristics, then the questionnaire concluded that the project was probably an agile-driven project. On the other hand, if the majority of the responses seemed to point towards a plan-driven methodology, then the questionnaire inferred that the project probably used a plan-driven software development methodology. By making these inferences, this data were included in the study even though a participant could not specifically identify the software development methodology employed.

Customer Satisfaction

Because customer satisfaction was the dependent variable, the key was to look at the project from a variety of angles, to understand why and how the project satisfied the customer. In measuring customer satisfaction, the questions inquired about how likely the firm would employ the stated project method (i.e., agile-driven or plan-driven) in future projects and how the project compared to similar projects of more or less the same size. Finally, given the quality, cost, and the ability of the project to meet its schedule, the respondents were asked about the value of project, and if it was a poor, good, or an excellent value for the money.

Product Quality

Hayes (1998) observed that product quality consisted of the characteristics listed in Table 1. There were eight questions in this section of the survey, but there are nine issues listed in the table. Because there was one question for each issue, the only issue that was not included in the survey was inter-operability. The reason was because inter-operability deals with the interrelationships among projects being executed concurrently. The issue is impossible to measure when collecting the data at the end of the software development life cycle. By ignoring the issue of inter-operability, there could have been some internal validity issues at stake; however, the effect probably dissipated after the project was completed.

Project Team Effectiveness

In order to determine if agile-driven software development methodology satisfied the customer, project team effectiveness was examined from a variety of angles. From one perspective, the confidence that the consumer or a stakeholder had in the project team, and the perceived ability of the project team to address issues needed to be studied (Spunt, 1999). From another viewpoint, project team effectiveness was concerned with the responsiveness of the team, the speed at which issues were resolved, the availability of the team, and the professionalism and enthusiasm of the team members (Hayes, 1998). The idea was to measure not only the ability of the project team to meet customer goals, but also the perceived desire of the team to satisfy customers.

Project Management Effectiveness

The third variable considered was project management effectiveness. Because product quality was the first independent variable, the two remaining factors that determined project management effectiveness were the ability to complete the project on time and the ability to complete the project on or under budget (Kertzner, 2001). The two constructs were plan-driven project management issues, and are discussed in all texts that deal extensively with project management.

Potential Problems with the Project

In this section in the survey, the customer provided data on problems with the project that were not captured by the existing or corresponding constructs. The section was included in the survey because it highlighted common problems that occurred in a software development project. Question 42 listed 16 potential issues, where in the last option a participant could confirm that no serious problems were encountered. If a serious problem did crop up in the project, then the participant was asked if he or she discussed the problem with the project manager, if he or she discussed the issue with someone other than the project manager, and if the concern was resolved to the participant's satisfaction.

Demographic Information

The purpose of this section of the survey was to collect data on the individual taking the survey. The questions asked the respondents to reveal his or her occupational classification based on the classifications from the Bureau of Labor Statistics (2008). In total, 40 separate job classifications were available in a drop-down list box. If a participant did not find a job classification that fit his or her role, he or she had the opportunity to enter a specific job classification. The section also inquired of a participant how many years he or she had been engaged in the job classification selected in the previous question. A participant was also asked to characterize the role that he or she played in the project. Questions 49 and 50 asked about the approximate age and gender of a participant. Question 51 allowed a participant to enter additional comments.

Thank You for Your Participation

In this section of the questionnaire, the survey thanked a respondent for his or her participation. The instructions in the beginning of the questionnaire were described again in chiasmic style, pointing out that the data that were collected would be held in strict confidence and that it would not be possible to identify the responses from specific individuals. It was also stated that the responses collected from this questionnaire would be used for a doctoral dissertation, and that the results of the analysis could appear in a academic or trade publication. Finally, a participant was informed that if he or she pressed the *Submit Your Responses* button, then that individual was giving his or her consent to include the data in the study. In the last sentence, a respondent was again thanked for his or her participation.

Selection of the Participants

Seven individuals verified the questionnaire that appears in Appendix C, where five of these people had attained terminal degrees in business management and were competent in project management, software development, and/or survey construction. The sixth person earned a masters degree in electrical engineering, and had over 30 years of paid professional experience in project management and software development. The last individual earned a bachelor's degree in English and master's degree in social work, and was selected because of her ability to formulate succinct English questions and sentences.

Because of the difficulty in finding companies that would be willing to allow their employees to be interviewed, it was decided to post the letter in Appendix B on the relevant Google.com user groups, the Yahoo.com user groups, and contact the various System Process Improvement Networks (SPINs) associated with the Software Engineering Institute (SEI). The letter in Appendix B was posted on 51 different Google.com user groups, but it was not possible to determine how many individuals belonged to any given user group. The letter was also posted on 116 different Yahoo.com user groups with 136,095 potential participants. Of the 116 Yahoo.com user groups, 45 national and international user groups were associated with the Project Management Institute (PMI), and had 39,209 potential participants. Thirdly, the SPIN user groups in the Directory of System Process Improvement Networks listed on the Software Engineering Institute web site were used. Forty SPIN user groups located in the United States were sent the letter contained in Appendix B, whereas 87 international SPIN user groups were also contacted. The SEI web site did not possess any information regarding the number of members in any given local SPIN user group. The email was sent to the contact person listed on SEI web site. At least two attempts were made to contact the various user groups mentioned above. The frequency of contact ranged from one week to three weeks. There were 185 individuals who responded to the survey.

The data were collected via the internet, and when a respondent completed the questionnaire, the answers were stored in a Golden Hills Software database. SurveyGold then sent an email indicating that new data had arrived, and were ready to be downloaded and viewed. On reading the email, the data were downloaded to this researcher's computer. The data stored on the Golden Hills Software database were logically deleted. At the end of each day, the data in the Golden Hills Software database were physically deleted, and thus no longer accessible.

Procedures

Because the purpose of a project is to achieve a specified objective in a limited amount of time, and because it is difficult to capture the characteristics of a project when it is executing, a project was evaluated after it was completed. Rising and Derby (2003), as well as Chin (2004), wrote that by incorporating a retrospective analysis at the end of an iteration, team members were better equipped to see a project in its totality, thus ensuring that these individuals work together effectively.

According to the Project Management Institute, there are five major and overlapping processes in a project, including the initiation processes, the planning processes, the executing processes, the controlling processes, and the closing processes (PMBOK Guide, 2005). The initiation processes authorize the project, whereas planning processes define and refine the project's objectives and goals. The executing processes coordinate the people and the resources. The controlling processes ensure that the objectives and goals were being met, and the closing processes formalize the acceptance of the result, bringing the project to its conclusion (Gray & Larson, 2006). At the end of each process, a certain amount of introspection occurs to assure that the process was successful. The analysis is concerned with the quality of the product, the effectiveness of the project team, and the effectiveness of the project management. Thus, it made sense to measure these issues at the end of a project life cycle.

SurveyGold Software Package

The SurveyGold Standard edition is a software package that helps in the building and administering surveys, as well as in analyzing results. It is suited for individuals, academic institutions and organizations that need to create and conduct surveys over the web, on the phone, or in a printed questionnaire form (SurveyGold, 2008). The software application uses point-and-click features to generate and carry out surveys. SurveyGold assigns point values for each question, and has the ability to score automatically the responses of every respondent (SurveyGold, 2008). The software can also collect web survey responses without establishing a subscription account or incurring a processing charge per response. SurveyGold can merge responses into its database to be viewed and analyzed using a variety of colors and fonts (SurveyGold, 2008). Because no prior knowledge of web design or HTML is necessary, the application can assign point values to create an optimal response. SurveyGold also has the ability to score survey results automatically, and to generate cross tabulation tables and frequency charts. Finally, the response data can be converted to Data Interchange Format (DIF), dBase, Excel, Hypertext Markup Language (HTML), Statistical Package for the Social Sciences (SPSS), or text formats (SurveyGold, 2008). There is a choice of having one respondent per record or one response per record (SurveyGold, 2008).

Round Trip Web Surveys

Set Up the Web Survey. The questions on customer satisfaction were devised from studying the customer satisfaction questions contained in Spunt (1999). The information in Hayes (1998) formed the basis of the product quality questions. Kerzner (2006) was particularly useful in generating questions on project team effectiveness and project management effectiveness. This author was responsible for constructing the project and participant demographics questions. The questions were then entered into the SurveyGold software application along with the associated responses (SurveyGold, 2008).

Publish the Web Survey. The next step was to publish the web survey. In other words, the questionnaire was saved as a web form and then it was imported into Web Studio 4.0 from Back to the Beach Software, LLC (Web Studio 4.0, 2008). Potential participants were sent the email contained in Appendix B. The individual then clicked on the survey hyperlink (i.e., http://www.assessingagilepm.com), and the survey appeared in a window of his or her browser. By clicking on the button entitled: *Proceed to take the questionnaire*, a respondent began to answer the survey questions. The survey was never distributed as an email attachment or in printed form.

   Participants Enter Responses. When a respondent finished answering all of the survey questions, he or she merely clicked on the button entitled: *Submit Your Responses* that appeared at the end of the questionnaire. If at any time while taking the questionnaire a respondent decided not to participate, he or she needed to only close the window, and the data were not collected. SurveyGold had no per response processing fees, no time limits, and no limits on the number of respondents (SurveyGold, 2008). The only optional question in the survey was the last question where a respondent was asked if he or she wanted to provide any additional comments.

   Gather the Responses. Survey responses were collected temporarily on the SurveyGold.com web site. This researcher was notified by email when new responses arrived on the SurveyGold web site, and were ready to be downloaded for analysis (SurveyGold, 2008).

   Download the Responses. By clicking the *Get Responses* button contained in the *Conduct Survey* tab of SurveyGold, the application automatically downloaded the new survey responses. At the end of the day, these new responses were permanently from the SurveyGold database (SurveyGold, 2008). The download process collected the responses, and presented the cumulative data to be viewed and analyzed on the researcher's personal computer.

   View and Analyze the Responses. SurveyGold was used to view and initially analyze the data. The application permitted the researcher to convert the data into SPSS format. After the conversion process was completed, the data file was used as input to the Statistical Package for the Social Sciences (SurveyGold, 2008).

Discussion of Data Processing

Data Collection

   The research employed the survey that is presented in Appendix C. The letter contained in Appendix B was emailed to 51 different Google.com user groups, 116 different Yahoo.com user groups, 50 SPIN organizations in the United States, and 87 SPIN organizations located internationally. Of the 116 Yahoo.com user groups contacted, 45 of these user groups were associated with the Project Management Institute. As suggested by Hayes (1998), the survey questions for the dependent variable and the independent variables were grouped together in the questionnaire. Once a participant submitted their responses to the survey, SurveyGold wrote a cookie to the participant's personal computer, thereby preventing him or her from taking the survey multiple times (SurveyGold, 2008).

Once the data were collected and converted into SPSS format, a variety of frequency tables were generated using the SPSS software application. Frequency tables were created for the entire data set, followed by frequency tables based on whether the respondents provided data on an agile-driven software development project, on a plan-driven software driven project, or if the respondent did not know which software development methodology was employed. Of the 185 respondents to the questionnaire, 95 were affiliated with known agile-driven projects, 53 were involved with plan-driven projects, and 37 individuals did not know what software development methodology was used in the creation of the software product under consideration. Each one of these 37 people answered a series of three questions in order to categorize whether the project had possibly been agile-driven or plan-driven. It was inferred that 24 of the 37 respondents reported on probable agile-driven software development projects, and 13 respondents provided data on probable plan-driven software development projects. Once the probable agile-driven and plan-driven software development projects were isolated, a Chow (1960) test conducted. The F-statistics were statistically insignificant at the 95% confidence level, implying that the known agile-driven projects could be pooled with the probable agile-driven projects, and the known plan-driven projects could be combined with the probable plan-driven projects.

Characteristics of the Projects

A major criticism that could be levied against this study by the agile-driven community is that the agile-driven projects studied herein were not representative of agile-driven software development projects experienced by the community. In other words, the project data that formed the basis of this study somehow skewed the result, and that customer satisfaction is indeed significantly greater for agile-driven projects than for plan-driven projects. In order to address this potential criticism, the participants answered six questions on the characteristics of the projects, including questions on the number of person hours expended, the number of project team members, the budgeted dollar amounts for a project, how long ago was a project completed, the estimated duration of a project, and the actual duration of a project. The actual dollars spent on a project was not asked of the participants because Fleming and Koppleman (2000), Kerzner (2006), Meredith and Mantel (2003), and Schwalbe (2006) all agreed that in the information technology industry, the tracking of actual costs is an anathema. In order to calculate what was thought to be an accurate estimate of actual costs, the risk factors suggested by Cooper et al. (2005) were employed. The results in the succeeding chapter indicated that the projects contained in this study appeared to be representative agile-driven and plan-driven software development projects.

Characteristics of the Participants

Demographic data were also gathered on the participants. The respondents answered five demographic questions, including questions on his or her occupational classification, the number of years he or she was engaged in the selected occupation, the major role played that he or she in the project, the approximate age of the participant, and the gender of the participant. The data revealed the participants appeared to be homogeneous when subdivided by the software development methodology employed, except that at the 99% confidence level, individuals that were engaged in plan-driven software development projects were significantly older than individuals involved with agile-driven software development projects.

Cronbach's Alpha Calculations

SPSS was used to calculate the Cronbach's alpha values for customer satisfaction, product quality, project team effectiveness, and project management effectiveness. The data were subdivided by whether the software development methodology was known by a participant, by whether the software development methodology was inferred by this study, and by whether the known plus inferred software development methodologies were pooled together. For customer satisfaction, questions 12, 15, 16, and 17 in the questionnaire were removed to achieve the highest positive Cronbach's alpha values. For product quality, project team effectiveness, and project management effectiveness, there was no need to remove any question when calculating the largest positive Cronbach's alpha value. However, for project management effectiveness the responses for questions 39 and 40 in the questionnaire were mirror imaged to ensure that the Cronbach's alpha values were indeed positive. The results are contained in Table 2.

Aside from the Cronbach's alpha values for project management effectiveness, all but one of the values were greater than .700. According to Cronbach (1951), for each variable, the subset of questions that were selected would reliably estimate the values of customer satisfaction, product quality, and project team effectiveness. As for project management effectiveness, all of the Cronbach's alpha values were greater than .700, except for plan-driven software development projects only, again indicating a high degree of reliability. The Cronbach's alpha value for plan-driven software development projects only was .665, close enough to .700 to ensure that all four questions associated to project management effectiveness could be included in the analysis of the data.

Table 2 *Cronbach's Alpha Values for the Variables of the Model*

Software Development Methodology	Customer Satisfaction (5 Items)	Product Quality (7 Items)	Project Team Effectiveness (12 Items)	Project Management Effectiveness (4 Items)
All Projects	.893	.838	.927	.736
Known Agile-Driven Projects	.875	.836	.922	.760
Probable Agile Driven Projects	.717	.710	.942	.703
Known Agile-Driven plus Probable Agile-Driven Projects	.863	.827	.929	.708
Known Plan-Driven Projects	.927	.845	.929	.665
Probable Plan-Driven Projects	.896	.847	.901	.860
Known Plan-Driven plus Probable Plan-Driven Projects	.924	.848	.922	.708

Regression Equation

Because of the Cronbach's alpha values contained in Table 2 as well as the questions that were selected to remain, for each respondent an averaged value for customer satisfaction, product quality, project team effectiveness, and project management effectiveness was calculated. The results were then used as data in estimating the following multiple regression model:

$$CS = \beta_0 + \beta_1 DV + \beta_2 PQ + \beta_3 PTE + \beta_4 PME + \varepsilon$$

where CS = customer satisfaction, DV = dummy variable that equals zero for plan-driven software development projects and one for agile-driven software development projects, PQ = product quality, PTE = project team effectiveness, and PME = project management effectiveness. Note that β_0 is interpreted to be autonomous customer satisfaction for plan-driven software development projects, and β_1 is the contribution to autonomous customer satisfaction the occurred because of the use and results of employing agile-driven software development methods. Furthermore, if β_1 is statistically significant at the 95% or 99% confidence levels, then this indicates that the null hypothesis H0 that the customer satisfaction level for agile-driven software development projects equals the customer satisfaction level for plan-driven software development projects can be rejected.

It was assumed that ε is the random error such that $\varepsilon \sim N(0, \sigma^2)$. When estimating the multiple regression model above, two additional assumptions beyond $\varepsilon \sim N(0, \sigma^2)$ that were made regarding the model. First, the random variable ε was homoscedastic, and there was no serial correlation in the error term. Both of these assumptions made sense because a data point corresponded to different software development project.

Heteroscedasticity. The assumption of homoscedasticity means that the variation of each ε around its zero mean does not depend upon product quality, project team effectiveness, or project management effectiveness (Koutsoyiannis, 1977). In other words, the variance σ^2 is not constant, but can be expressed as a function of the explanatory variables. When such a functional relationship exists, heteroscedasticity is said to be present.

Autocorrelation. The fourth assumption of ordinary least squares is that successive values of the residuals are temporally independent, or that the covariance between any two residuals equals zero (Koutsoyiannis, 1977). Because a post-test experimental design method was employed and because each data point represented a different project, testing for the presence of autocorrelation was not relevant.

Multicollinearity. It is natural to encounter some multicollinearity among product quality, project team effectiveness, and project management effectiveness. The reason that multicollinearity exists is because product quality, project team effectiveness, and project management effectiveness are related to each other and move in unison (Kerzner, 2006). According to Aczel and Sounderpandian (2002), the effects of multicollinearity are manifold. First, the variances and standard errors of the regression coefficients could be inflated. Second, the magnitudes of the regression coefficients may not be as expected. Third, signs of the regression coefficients may be opposite of what is expected. Fourth, the adding or removing of variables may produce large changes in the coefficient estimates, including a change in the value of the respective signs (Aczel & Sounderpandian, 2002). Fifth, by removing a data point, the coefficient may change significantly. Sixth, the F-statistic of the regression equation may be statistically significant, whereas none of the t-statistics are statistically significant (Aczel & Sounderpandian, 2002).

According to Aczel and Sounderpandian (2002), a good solution to the problem of multicollinearity is to remove the offending explanatory variable from the regression equation. The idea is that because most of the explanatory power is contained in the other variables, the dropping of the appropriate explanatory variable will not significantly affect the size of R-square. In fact, if the adjusted R squared value actually increases when the multicollinear variable is removed, then this indicates that the decision was correct (Aczel & Sounderpandian, 2002). However, because product quality, project team effectiveness, and project management effectiveness are the theoretical explanatory variables as defined by the *Agile Manifesto*, it seemed that the limit of the research was to report on the presence of multicollinearity, and then possibly suggest some modifications to the theory if the level of multicollinearity was severe. Even so, it is the responsibility of the signers of the *Agile Manifesto* to modify the precepts of the document if it is deemed appropriate.

Methodological Assumptions and Limitations

Strengths and Weaknesses

The purpose of this section is to discuss the methodological assumptions, limitations, and delimitations. Thus, confounding, reliability, and validity are described in terms of product quality, project team effectiveness, and project management effectiveness.

Confounding. Because there was some multicollinearity present in the explanatory variables, it could be that product quality, project team effectiveness, and project management effectiveness were confounded. What is evident is that the three explanatory variables were related to each other. For example, correctness and reliability of the software product could be linked directly to usability, which in turn could be associated with how well the project team worked together and how well the project was managed. To address the needs of a customer, the project team could to respond in a timely manner so that product quality would be in alignment with the priorities established by project management. The notion of delivering a project to completion in a timely manner at an acceptable level of quality and hopefully on or under budget could have been responsible for the presence of multicollinearity.

Reliability. In developing the questionnaire in Appendix C, the purpose was to assess the level of customer satisfaction regardless of whether agile-driven software or plan-driven software development methods were employed. According to Hayes (1998), the three types of reliability are stability, equivalence, and internal consistency. The stability of customer satisfaction over time was dependent upon when the project was completed and when the questionnaire was taken (Hayes, 1998). If the time difference was relatively short, then the stability effects were probably minimal. If the time interval was relatively long, then stability and the reliability of customer satisfaction could have lowered the values of the correlation coefficients (Hayes, 1998). Because the same questionnaire was given to respondents who participated in either agile-driven or plan-driven software development projects, equivalence reliability was not an issue. Internal consistency was measured using Cronbach's alpha (Hayes, 1998). From Table 2, it was evident that the reliability estimates were quite high, where all but one of the statistics were greater than .700.

Validity. According to Trochim (2001), the four types of validity issues are conclusion validity, internal validity, construct validity, and external validity. Conclusion validity asks whether there was a relationship between product quality, project team effectiveness, project management effectiveness and customer satisfaction (Cozby, 2004). For a customer to be satisfied the final software product must have been of an acceptable level of quality, independent of whether agile or plan-driven software development methods were employed. Second, the project team must have worked together closely, being responsive to customer needs. Third, the project management must have been able to complete the project at on time and on or under budget. Thus, it appeared that conclusion validity holds, or a relationship exists between product quality, project team effectiveness, project management effectiveness, and customer satisfaction.

According to Trochim (2001), a design is susceptible to a variety of threats to internal validity. A historical threat can exist if some historical event affects the outcome of the study (Trochim, 2001). Maturation, mortality, and selection threats did not exist because the study used a post-test only methodology (Trochim, 2001). A regression threat is a statistical phenomenon that can occur because the participants do not randomly choose to respond to the questionnaire (Trochim, 2001). This may have been the reason for the presence of some multicollinearity in the explanatory variables. Construct validity is concerned with how well the operational model measure the theoretical model (Cozby, 2004). Given Kerzner's (2006) discussion on what constitutes a successful project, it appeared that construct validity was not an issue. External validity involves generalizing the results of the study to other people, places, times, and projects (Trochim, 2001). The questionnaire listed in Appendix C could be easily have been used in studying other software development projects. The issues that could affect external validity would be the project selected by a participant, the size of a project, the number of team members, the cost of a project, the duration of a project, and/or the complexity of a project. Other factors that could have threatened external validity are the culture of an organization or when the project was done. Because a post-test methodology was used, there was little if anything that could have been done to mitigate these potential external threats.

Ethical Assurances

Each of the issues regarding ethically responsible research are examined in turn, linking the research with the appropriate ethical concern.

Informed Consent

Smith (2000) stated that researchers should respect human participants because he or she were worthy of respect, regardless of their immaturity, incapacitation, or any other circumstances that limit his or her liberty, independence, and freedom. A questionnaire should include an unambiguous statement of the purposes, procedures, risks, and benefits, as well as the obligations and commitments of both the participants and the researcher, because individuals should be treated as free and competent agents (Fischman, 2000).

The consent form consisted of a short paragraph of text at both the beginning and end of the questionnaire, asking a respondent to participate in the survey. It did not replace the consent process, where a participant would have been encouraged to ask questions, request clarification, and consider what was presented (Fischman, 2000). By starting to answer the survey questions, a respondent was initially agreeing to participate in the survey. By pressing the *Submit Your Responses* button at the end of the questionnaire, a respondent gave his or her informed consent (Sieber, 2000).

Beneficence and Non-malfeasance

When planning and conducting research involving human participants, Smith (2000) suggested the researcher is responsible for maximizing the possible benefits, and minimizing the potential costs, or harm, to the participants. This moral principle is utilitarian and straightforward in nature (Smith, 2000). The problem is that it was difficult to gauge the potential costs and benefits in advance by calculating a benefit/cost ratio, weighing the costs incurred by a participant against the potential gains to science, or to society as a whole (Smith, 2000). The question was how to ascribe benefits and costs in quantitatively measurable terms, such as in dollars or some other objective units of measure.

Types of Risks. Although taking the survey may have inconvenienced a participant, because it was an internet-based survey, the assumption was that participants answered the survey questions at a convenient time, only incurring an opportunity cost. There was no physical risk in taking the survey. Because customer satisfaction is subjective in nature, there was a possibility that a participant would use the survey as a vehicle for venting feelings of frustration and anger. One form of social risk may have been present was the rejection by a participant's peers. Although this risk was probably minimal, or even non-existent, a participant could have taken the survey, expressing his or her feelings without fear of exposure. A respondent did not incur an economic risk or a legal risk because it was impossible to identify any given individual.

Benefits of Research. Because an internet survey was employed, any relationship between a participant and the researcher was probably at best transitory or at worst non-existent. The knowledge gained by understanding whether agile-driven software development methods were beneficial could definitely be important to a participant. The fact that the proponents of the agile-driven methodology espoused that the use and results of the method satisfied a customer was the issue under consideration. Any verification of this principle is definitely an important piece of information to a participant.

The prospect of doing good and receiving the esteem of others could be a benefit, particularly if it translated into continued employment and the possibility for advancement. It was probably not be an issue in taking this survey. However, participation in the survey may have triggered a desire by a respondent to think critically about agile-driven and plan-driven software development methods. Personal and/or political empowerment of this author was not an issue. Finally, there is the benefit accrued to the agile-driven software development community. Because the results indicated that autonomous customer satisfaction was not statistically significant at the 99% confidence level, the study did not confirm a major precept of the *Agile Manifesto*. However, when the software development methodology employed was either known or inferred, the amount of additional autonomous customer satisfaction for agile-driven software development projects was barely statistically significant at the 95% confidence level.

Justice

According to the Compact Oxford English Dictionary (2003), justice is the quality of being just or "the administration of law or some other authority according to the principles of just behavior and treatment" (p. 608). First, it was assumed that there was no significant power differential between the participants and the researcher because it was a straightforward process to collect data. Second, because procedural justice is concerned with the fairness of the research process, every effort was made to ensure that a participant had sufficient information to provide his or her informed consent without experiencing undue stress or duress.

Trust

Trust is a "firm belief in the reliability, truth, ability, or strength of someone or something" (Compact Oxford English Dictionary, 2003, p. 1238). It is also being responsible for someone or something, where a person assumes nominal responsibility on behalf of one or more individuals. Because a participant was doing this researcher a favor by responding to the questionnaire, he or she was treated with respect, and was never the object of demeaning conversation.

Safety of Participants. The federal regulations that protect human participants specifically state that when appropriate the research plan should monitor the data being collected to ensure the safety of the participants (Eyde, 2000). Because there was no physical risk, there seemed to be no physical or psychological harm to the participants.

Withdrawal Rights. According to Eyde (2000), autonomy requires that a participant have the right to withdraw his or her data, whereas the fidelity to science principle would claim just the opposite. A participant had the right to withdraw his or her data after having taken the survey prior to pressing the *Submit Your Response* button at the end of the questionnaire by merely closing the survey window. None of the participants have requested that his or her data be removed from this study.

Changes in IRB Protocol. There were no changes in the IRB protocol during the course of the study.

Debriefing. According to Eyde (2000), a researcher should debrief a participant immediately after having participated in the study, or shortly thereafter, depending upon the nature of the research. At the end of the questionnaire, a participant had the opportunity to read a short debriefing paragraph. It pointed out that the data collected would be held in strict confidence and that it would not be possible to identify the responses from specific individuals. It was also stated that the data collected would be used for a doctoral dissertation, and that the results of the analysis could appear in a academic or trade publication. Finally, a participant was informed that if he or she pressed the *Submit Your Responses* button, then he or she was giving his or her consent to include the data in the study. A respondent was thanked a second time for his or her participation.

Deception. The intent of the research was not to deceive a participant. Any opinions regarding agile-driven or plan-driven software development methods were assumed to have been previously formed in the minds of the participants.

Fidelity to Science

Smith (2000) aptly perceived that researchers are dedicated to the discovery and propagation of truth. For the purposes of this study, fidelity to science was a matter of curiosity. It was felt that the topic of customer satisfaction regarding the use and results of agile-driven and plan-driven software development methods was worthy of investigation. The protagonists in the field believe that agile-driven methods are conducive to satisfying customers. The fact that apparently no one has of yet statistically verified that the use and results of agile-driven methods satisfy customers means that it needs to be investigated. Thus, the propagation of truth was the issue that was worthy of discovery and effort.

Ethical Conflicts

No matter how much a researcher attempts to be honest, just and fair, ethical conflicts may appear. Even with the approval from the IRB, the value of the study should not be over-estimated, nor should the ethical liabilities be underestimated.

Conflicting Roles. Because the data were collected via an internet survey, there was no opportunity for role conflict to occur, and no role conflicts did occur.

Resolving Ethical Dilemmas. During the course of collecting the data for this study, no ethical dilemmas appeared on the scene.

CHAPTER 4 - FINDINGS

Overview

In this chapter, the types of software development methodologies chosen by the participants in the study are discussed, including a variety of agile-driven methods, an assortment of plan-driven methods, and whether a respondent knew what particular software development method was used. For the 37 participants who did not know what methodology was employed, a series of three questions were asked about the project characterization, the project environment, and the project management. By invoking a majority rule, it was inferred whether one of these 37 projects was either probably agile-driven or probably plan-driven. Two Chow (1960) tests were performed using the data from known agile-driven projects and probable agile-driven projects as well as from known plan-driven projects and the probable plan-driven projects. In both cases, the F-statistics were statistically insignificant at the 95% confidence level, implying that the data could be pooled forming two sets, known agile-driven plus probable agile-driven projects and known plan-driven plus probable plan-driven projects.

The six project characteristics are examined, including the number of person hours expended, the number of project team members, the budgeted dollar amounts for a project, how long ago was a project completed, the estimated project duration, and the actual project duration. The five participant characteristics are scrutinized, including occupational classification, the number years engaged in that occupation, the major role played in the project, the approximate age of a participant, and the gender of a participant. The means, medians and standard deviations for the characteristics of the projects and the characteristics of the participants are analyzed.

Furthermore, the counts and the percentages of the most significant problem encountered by a participant are reported. Of the pre-defined responses for question 42, the most common issue was that the project specifications were not clearly understood by the project team. This problem occurred for both known agile-driven plus probable agile-driven projects and for known plan-driven plus probable plan-driven projects. For both methodologies, the participants also provided unique problems not included in the set of pre-defined responses. These other issues are listed in Table 26 for known agile-driven plus probable agile-driven projects and in Table 27 for known plan-driven plus probable plan-driven projects.

The results of four regressions are presented. The data for the first regression included those projects where the software development methodology was known by the participants. Along with product quality, project team effectiveness, and project management effectiveness, a dummy variable was used, where it equaled zero for known plan-driven projects and one for known agile-driven projects. Because the non-standardized coefficient for the dummy variable was not statistically significant at the 95% confidence level, the second regression only contained the three explanatory variables. Both regressions employed a constant term representing autonomous customer satisfaction. The constant term and the coefficients for the explanatory variables were statistically significant at the 99% confidence level.

Because the two Chow (1960) tests indicated that the projects where the software development was known could be pooled with the projects where the software development methodology was inferred, the third and fourth regression used all 185 data points. The third regression contained a dummy variable, where the value of the dummy variable was zero for known plan-driven plus probable plan-driven projects and one for known agile-driven plus probable plan driven projects. In this regression, the coefficient of the dummy variable was barely statistically significant at the 95% confidence level, but not statistically significant at the 99% confidence level. This is an important result, and it is argued in the analysis section of this chapter that because customer satisfaction, product quality, project team effectiveness, and project management effectiveness contained averaged values, the 99% confidence level was the more appropriate significance level to employ. The fourth regression used the same data as the third regression, but the dummy variable was removed. In both the third and fourth regressions, the constant term and the coefficients for the explanatory variables were statistically significant at the 99% confidence level.

In the analysis section of this chapter, it is observed that the characteristics of the projects conformed to the conventional wisdom regarding agile-driven and plan-driven projects (Boehm & Turner, 2004; Highsmith, 2004; Schwaber, 2004). In other words, agile-driven projects were significantly smaller than plan-driven projects in terms of the number person hours expended, the number of team members, and budgeted dollar amounts. For example, for known agile-driven plus probable agile-driven projects, the mean number of person hours expended was 2,303 person hours, the average number of project team members was 7.9 individuals, and the typical budgeted dollar amount was $155,455. On the average, a known agile-driven or probable agile-driven project was completed 3.8 months prior to a participant taking the survey, the mean estimated project duration was 7.0 months, and the average actual project duration was 7.9 months. In contrast, for known plan-driven plus probable plan-driven projects, the mean number of person hours expended was 5,273 person hours, the average number of project team members was 16.7 individuals, and the typical budgeted dollar amount was $238, 630. On the average, a project was completed 7.6 months prior to a participant taking the survey, the mean estimated project duration was 8.4 months, and the average actual project duration was 7.1 months. These results appeared to confirm the conventional wisdom regarding the characteristics of agile-driven and plan-driven software development projects.

The characteristics of the participants is also reviewed. For both known agile-driven plus probable agile-driven projects, and for known plan-driven plus probable plan-driven projects, financial operations, computer, and mathematical occupations were the most common occupations, where the percentages were 38.7% and 25.8% respectively. The mean number of years for participants involved in both known agile-driven plus probable agile-driven projects and known plan-driven plus probable plan-driven projects was 8.1 years. When the major role of the respondents was examined, the project manager role had the most number of participants with 23.4% for known agile-driven plus probable agile-driven projects and 25.9% for known plan-driven plus probable plan-driven projects. The approximate age for respondents that who reported data on known agile-driven plus probable agile-driven projects was 34.8 years, whereas the approximate age of individuals who were associated with known plan-driven plus probable plan-driven projects was 37.1 years. Finally, the distribution of the participants by gender was approximately the same with approximately 84% of the respondents being male, and 16% of the respondents being female. Thus, aside from the average age of the participants, the respondents appeared to be homogeneous.

The four regressions are particularly enlightening. The results indicated that if a participant knew precisely the software development methodology that was employed, then there was no statistical difference in autonomous customer satisfaction at the 95% confidence level, and thus it was not possible to reject the null hypothesis H0. On the other hand, when a respondent knew what software development methodology was used, or was uncertain of the methodology employed, there was barely a statistically significant difference at the 95% confidence level, but not at the 99% confidence level. Because the values of customer satisfaction, product quality, project team effectiveness, and project management effectiveness all contained averaged values, it is argued that the 99% confidence level is the more appropriate level of significance to use, and it is again concluded that the null hypothesis H0 could not be rejected. Furthermore, if the 99% confidence level is the inappropriate confidence level to employ, then given the estimated values of the non-standardized coefficients of the dummy variables, the maximum level of autonomous customer satisfaction for the use and results of agile-driven methods never exceeded one, regardless of the data set examined.

Findings

Software Development Methodologies

The purpose of this section is to present and discuss the characteristics of the software development projects that were the objects of the study. It includes the type of software development methodology employed if it was known, and it was not known, it includes the probable software development methodologies used.

All of the Projects. The second question in the survey asked a respondent if the project was agile-driven, project-driven, or if he or she did not know the software development methodology that was employed. Table 3 contains these results. Ninety-five or 51.4% of the respondents claimed that the project under consideration used agile-driven software development methods, 53 or 28.6% of the respondents believed that the project employed plan-driven software development methods, and 37 or 20.0% of the respondents did not know what software development method was used. The third option was significant because it may have indicated that the software development methodology was less important than other project characteristics, such as the quality of the software project, the effectiveness of the project team, and the effectiveness of the project management.

Table 3 *Software Development Methodologies Used*

Software Development Methodologies	Count	Percent	Cumulative Percent
Agile-Driven Software Development Methodologies	95	51.4	51.4
Plan-Driven Software Development Methodologies	53	28.6	80.0
Unknown Software Development Methodologies	37	20.0	100.0
Total	185	100.0	

Agile-Driven Methodologies. Because there were a variety of agile-driven and plan-driven software development methods, the next series of questions asked a respondent to specify the software development methodology employed. For agile projects, Boehm and Turner (2004) identified seven different agile software development methods, including: (a) Extreme Programming, (b) Adaptive Software Development, (c) Crystal Methods, (d) Scrum, (e) Feature Driven Development, (f) Dynamic Systems Development, and (g) Lean Development. The questionnaire added two additional options; namely, it asked a participant if another agile-driven method was used but not listed, or if the respondent knew that an agile-driven method was used, but he or she was not aware of the name of that agile-driven method. In total, question three contained nine options. Table 4 provides a breakdown of the different agile-driven software development methods that were specified in the data.

Table 4 *Agile-Driven Software Development Methodologies Used*

Agile-Driven Software Development Methodologies	Count	Percent	Cumulative Percent
Extreme Programming	12	12.6	12.6
Adaptive Software Development	2	2.1	14.7
Scrum	58	61.1	75.8
Feature Driven Development	4	4.2	80.0
Lean Development	2	2.1	82.1
Other Agile-Driven Methodologies	9	9.5	91.6
Unknown Agile-Driven Methodology	8	8.4	100.0
Total	95	100.0	

Note. There were no responses for Crystal Methods and Dynamic Systems Development methodologies.

None of the participants were engaged in software development projects that used Crystal Methods or Feature Driven Development methods. Given that a large number of Google.com and Yahoo.com user groups were contacted, this probably meant that these two agile-driven software development methodologies were not popular among the members of the agile-driven community. The second feature of Table 4 is that 58 participants from Scrum projects decided to participate in the survey. This was significant, because may mean that the agile-driven software development community is congregating around Scrum, and thus this methodology is dominating agile-driven software development. Third, nine participants started that some other agile-driven software development methodology was used and that eight participants were aware that an agile-driven methodology was employed, but did not know its name. When examining the nine other listed agile-driven methodologies, no discernible pattern emerged. Even so, slightly over 80% of the respondents who were affiliated with agile-driven projects knew the name of the software development methodology used.

Table 5 *Plan-Driven Software Development Methodologies Used*

Plan-Driven Software Development Methodologies	Count	Percent	Cumulative Percent
Military Standards	1	1.9	1.9
ISO Standard	6	11.3	13.2
EIA Standard	2	3.8	17.0
IEEE Standard	2	3.8	20.8
Software Factory	5	9.4	30.2
Capability Maturity Model	3	5.7	35.9
Capability Maturity Model Integration	12	22.6	58.5
Personal Software Process	2	3.8	62.3
Team Software Process	11	20.8	83.0
Other Plan-Driven Methodology	4	7.5	90.6
Unknown Plan-Driven Methodology	5	9.4	100.0
Total	53	100.0	

Note. There were no responses for the Cleanroom Methodology.

Plan-Driven Methodologies. In contrast, Boehm and Turner (2004) discussed ten plan-driven software development methodologies, including: (a) Military Standards, (b) ISO Standard, (c) EIA Standard, (d) IEEE Standard, (e) Software Factory, (f) Cleanroom Methodology, (g) Capability Maturity, (h) Capability Maturity Model Integration, (i) Personal Software Process, and (j) Team Software Process. Again, the questionnaire added two additional options; namely, it asked a participant if another plan-driven method was employed that was not listed above, or if the respondent knew that a plan-driven method was used, but he or she was not aware of the name of that plan-driven method. Table 5 lists the different plan-driven software development methods that appeared in the data.

First, even though an attempt was made to collect plan-driven data from a variety of sources, no Cleanroom Methodology data are contained in Table 5. Second, because the Capability Maturity Model, the Capability Maturity Model Integration, the Personal Software Process, and the Team Software Process all originated at Carnegie-Mellon , these four plan-driven software development methodologies can be considered a variation on a single theme, and can be analyzed as a group in contrast to other plan-driven software development methodologies (Humphrey, 1999; Paulk et al., 1994). In fact, these four plan-driven software development methodologies constitute 52.8% of all of the plan-driven data collected. Finally, four participants stated the plan-driven software development methodology used was different than what was listed in the questionnaire, whereas five of the participants knew that the software development methodology used was plan-driven, but were not aware of what specific methodology was employed.

Unknown Methodologies. The last entry in Table 3 is the unknown software development methodologies. In this case, 37 participants did not know what software development methodology was used in the project under consideration. Three additional questions (i.e., 3a, 3b, and 3c) were asked of each of these respondents. The first question characterized a project by whether it exhibited rapid value and responsiveness to change as a means to an end, or if the project was predictable, stable, and a high assurance existed to anchor project processes, indicating an agile-driven project, whereas the second answer pointed to a project that was probably plan-driven. The second question discussed the environment of the project. The first possibility asked if the project existed in a turbulent high-change environment with some risks, whereas the second possibility asked if the requirements were determined in advance and remained relatively stable. The first option indicated an agile-driven project, whereas the second option pointed to a plan-driven project. The third question talked about the management of the project. In the first case, the project could be construed to be agile-driven if there was a dependence on dedicated customer representatives, whereas the project could be considered to be plan-driven if there was a dependence on some form of contract between the project team and the customers. Finally, if at least two out of the three responses were answered along agile-driven lines, then it was inferred that the software development project was probably agile-driven. If at least two out of the three responses pointed to a plan-driven project, then it was inferred that the project was probably a plan-driven software development project. Table 6 provides the breakdown

between probable agile-driven software development projects and probable plan-driven
software development projects.

Table 6 *Unknown Software Development Methodologies Used*

Inferred Software Development Methodologies	Count	Percent	Cumulative Percent
Probable Agile-Driven Methodologies	24	64.9	64.9
Probable Plan-Driven Methodologies	13	35.1	100.00
Total	37	100.0	

An obvious result from Table 6 is that when the software development methodology
was not known, approximately two-thirds (i.e., 64.9%) of these projects were probably agile-
driven, whereas about one-third (i.e., 35.1%) of these projects were probably plan-driven.
When examining the data from Table 3, there were 95 specified agile-driven software
development projects and 53 known plan-driven software development projects, or 64.2%
agile-driven software development projects and 35.8% plan-driven software development
projects. In other words, the ratios of agile-driven to plan-driven software development
projects were approximately the same.

Pooling Data Issues. In order to decide whether pooled data were appropriate to use
in the study, two Chow (1960) tests were conducted using the known agile-driven plus
probable agile-driven data as well as using the known plan-driven plus probable plan-driven
data. According to Koutsoyiannis (1977), for the Chow (1960) test, a regression is calculated
for the pooled data, followed by two regressions one for each of two samples. In this case,
two regressions were computed using the agile-driven plus probable agile-projects, and then
another regression employing the known plan-driven plus probable plan-driven projects. In
the next step, one regression was generated using the known agile-driven projects and another
regression was created using the probable agile-driven projects. Two more regressions were
calculated, one employing the known plan-driven projects and another employing the
probable plan-driven projects. The number of data points, the sum of squares of the residuals,
and the degrees of freedom for six regressions are contained in Table 7. Two *F*-statistics were
computed, one for the known agile-driven plus probable agile-driven projects, and a second
for the known plan-driven plus probable plan-driven projects. For all six regressions, the
dependent variable was customer satisfaction, a constant term was included, and the

explanatory variables were product quality, project team effectiveness, and project management effectiveness.

When pooling the known agile-driven plus probable agile-driven projects, the calculated F-statistic value for the Chow (1960) test was $F(4,111) = 2.891$, which was not statistically significant at the 95% confidence level, where the critical value for the F-statistic was 3.506 (Koutsoyiannis, 1977). When pooling the known plan-driven plus probable plan-driven projects, the F-statistic for the Chow (1960) test was $F(4,58) = .396$, which as not statistically significant at the 95% confidence level, where the critical value for the F-statistic was 3.668 (Koutsoyiannis, 1977).

Table 7 *Sum of Squares of the Residuals Used in the Two Chow Tests*

Agile-Driven Projects and Plan-Driven Projects	Count	Sums of Squares of the Residuals	Degrees of Freedom of the Residuals
Known Agile-Driven Projects	95	22.027	91
Probable Agile-Driven Projects	24	5.309	20
Known Agile-Driven plus Probable Agile-Driven Projects	119	30.184	115
Known Plan-Driven Projects	53	15.540	49
Probable Plan-Driven Projects	13	2.024	9
Known Plan-Driven plus Probable Plan-Driven Projects	66	18.044	62

Note. Customer satisfaction was the dependent variable, and product quality, project team effectiveness, and project management effectiveness were the explanatory variables.

Because both F-statistics from the two Chow (1960) tests were statistically insignificant at the 95% confidence level, it meant that the known agile-driven projects could be pooled with the probable agile-driven projects, and that the known plan-driven projects could be pooled with the probable plan-driven projects. Had either one or both of the F-statistics been statistically significant at the 95% confidence level, it would not have made sense to pool the known agile-driven projects with probable agile-driven projects or the known agile-driven projects with the probable agile-driven projects, and thus the findings would have been different.

Characteristics of the Projects

Questions four through nine of the survey were concerned with characterizing the projects that made up the study. Question four attempted to discover the number of person hours expended by a project, and question five addressed the number of individuals or project team members. Question six dealt with the budget for a project. Finally, questions eight and nine asked about the estimated and actual project durations respectively.

Table 8 *Number of Person Hours Expended*

Number of Person Hours Expended	All Projects	Known Agile-Driven plus Probable Agile-Driven Projects	Known Plan-Driven plus Probable Plan-Driven Projects
	Count (Percent)	Count (Percent)	Count (Percent)
Under 1,000 person hours	44 (23.9%)	34 (28.6%)	10 (15.2%)
1,000-1,999	28 (15.1%)	23 (19.3%)	5 (7.6%)
2,000-3,999	25 (13.5%)	15 (12.6%)	10 (15.2%)
4,000-7,999	28 (15.1%)	19 (16.0%)	9 (13.6%)
8,000-11,999	18 (9.7%)	9 (7.6%)	9 (13.6%)
12,000-19,999	11 (5.9%)	4 (3.3%)	7 (10.6%)
20,000 or over person hours	31 (16.8%)	15 (12.6%)	16 (24.2%)
Total	185 (100.0%)	119 (100.0%)	66 (100.0%)

Size of the Projects. One of the major tenets of agile software development methods is that agile-driven methods work best in small projects (Highsmith, 2004; Schwaber, 2004). Question four of the survey in Appendix C attempted to verify this statement. The data presented in Table 8 compares all 185 projects in the survey, the known agile-driven plus probable agile-driven projects, and the known plan-driven plus probable plan-driven projects. Software development projects can be intuitively sub-divided into small-sized, medium-sized, and large-sized projects. For the purposes of this discussion, small-sized projects are projects that expended less than 2,000 person hours, medium-sized projects are projects that expended between 2,000 and 7,999 person hours, and large-sized projects are projects that expended 8,000 or more person hours. In Table 8, 38.9% of all projects were small-sized, whereas 28.6% were medium-sized, and 32.4% were large-sized. In other words, when all software development projects were considered, there seemed to be approximately a one-third, one-third, one-third split of the small-sized, medium-sized, and large-sized projects.

Table 8 contains 44 projects that expended less than 1,000 person hours of which 34 of these projects were known agile-driven or probable agile-driven, and 10 of the projects were known plan-driven or probable plan-driven. Of the 28 projects that expended between 1,000 and 1,999 person hours, 23 of the projects used known agile-driven or probable agile-driven software development methodologies, and five of the projects employed known plan-driven or probable plan-driven software development methodologies. Thus, 48.0% of all known agile-driven plus probable agile-driven projects were less than 2,000 person hours long, whereas 22.8% of all known plan-driven plus probable plan-driven projects were less than 2,000 person hours long. In other words, nearly half of the known agile-driven plus probable agile-driven projects contained in the survey were small-sized projects, whereas a little over a fifth of the known plan-driven plus probable plan-driven projects were small-sized projects.

Furthermore, of the 25 projects that expended between 2,000 and 3,999 person hours, 15 of the projects were known agile-driven or probable agile-driven, and the remaining 10 projects were known plan-driven or probable plan-driven. For the 28 projects that expended between 4,000 and 7,999 person hours, 19 of the projects were known agile-driven or probable agile-driven, and nine of the projects were known plan-driven or probable plan-driven. Thus, 28.6% of all known agile-driven plus probable agile-driven projects were medium-sized, whereas 28.8% of all known plan-driven plus probable plan-driven projects were medium sized projects.

As for the large-sized projects, 18 projects expended between 8,000 and 11,999 person hours, nine of the projects were agile-driven and nine of the projects were plan-driven. Of the 11 projects that expended between 12,000 and 19,999 person hours, four were agile-driven and seven were plan-driven. Finally, for the 31 projects that expended over 20,000 person hours, 15 of the projects were agile-driven and 16 of the projects were plan-driven. Thus, 23.5% of all known agile-driven plus probable agile-driven projects were large-sized projects, whereas 48.4% of all known plan-driven plus probable plan-driven projects were large-sized projects. Thus, it can be inferred from the data that agile-driven projects were more likely to be small-sized projects and plan-driven projects were more likely to be large-sized projects. In terms of the number of person hours expended by a project, little or nothing can be inferred about medium-sized projects.

Table 9 *Number of Project Team Members*

Number of Project Team Members	All Projects	Known Agile-Driven plus Probable Agile-Driven Projects	Known Plan-Driven plus Probable Plan-Driven Projects
	Count (Percent)	Count (Percent)	Count (Percent)
Under 10 people	95 (51.4%)	71 (59.7%)	24 (36.5%)
10 – 19 people	46 (24.9%)	24 (20.2%)	22 (33.3%)
20 – 39 people	17 (9.2%)	12 (10.1%)	5 (7.6%)
40 – 59 people	8 (4.3%)	6 (5.0%)	2 (3.0%)
60 – 79 people	6 (3.2%)	4 (3.4%)	2 (3.0%)
80 – 99 people	2 (1.1%)	0 (0.0%)	2 (3.0%)
100 people or over	11 (5.9%)	2 (1.6%)	9 (13.6%)
Total	185 (100.0%)	119 (100.0%)	66 (100.0%)

Another way to look at the pervasiveness of agile-driven methods is to examine the number of individuals who worked on the projects contained in the survey. Question five in the survey in Appendix C attempted to address this issue. Table 9 presents the raw data for all of the projects, the known agile-driven plus probable agile-driven projects, and the known plan-driven plus probable plan-driven projects. As in the previous sub-section, the number of project team members could be broken up into small-sized, medium-sized, and large-sized projects. In the discussion contained herein, it is posited that small-sized projects contained less than 10 team members, medium-sized projects possessed between 10 and 39 team members, and large-sized projects included 40 or more team members.

In Table 9, 95 of the projects used less than 10 team members of which 71 projects were known agile-driven or probable agile-driven, and 24 projects were known plan-driven or probable plan-driven. Of the 46 projects that employed between 10 and 19 team members, 24 projects were known agile-driven plus probable agile-driven projects, and 22 projects were known plan-driven or probable plan-driven. Furthermore, for the 17 projects that used between 20 and 39 individuals, 12 projects were known agile-driven or probable agile-driven, and five projects were known plan-driven or probable plan-driven. Finally, there were 27 projects that contained more than 40 team members of which 12 projects were known agile-driven or probable agile-driven, and 15 projects were known plan-driven or probable plan-driven.

Thus, 59.8% of all known agile-driven plus probable agile-driven projects could be construed to be small-sized projects, whereas 36.4% of all known plan-driven plus probable plan-driven projects could be classified as small-sized projects. Furthermore, 30.3% of all known agile-driven plus probable agile-driven projects were medium-sized projects, and 39.9% of all known plan-driven plus probable plan-driven projects were medium-sized projects. Finally, 10.0% of all known agile-driven plus probable agile- driven projects were inferred to be large-sized projects, and 19.6% of all known plan-driven plus probable plan-driven projects were considered to be large-sized projects. Thus, from the perspective of team membership, known agile-driven plus probable agile-driven projects seemed to be smaller than known plan-driven plus probable plan-driven projects.

Table 10 *Budgeted Dollar Amounts*

Budgeted Dollar Amounts	All Projects	Known Agile-Driven plus Probable Agile-Driven Projects	Known Plan-Driven plus Probable Plan-Driven Projects
	Count (Percent)	Count (Percent)	Count (Percent)
Under $50,000	44 (23.8%)	31 (26.1%)	13 (19.7%)
50,000 – 99,000	29 (15.7%)	20 (16.8%)	9 (13.6%)
100,000 – 249,999	18 (9.6%)	11 (9.2%)	7 (10.6%)
250,000 – 499,999	29 (15.7%)	21 (17.6%)	8 (12.1%)
500,000 – 999,999	21 (11.4%)	12 (10.1%)	9 (13.6%)
1,000, 000 – 4,999,999	25 (13.5%)	15 (12.6%)	10 (15.2%)
$5,000,000 or over	19 (10.3%)	9 (7.6%)	10 (15.2%)
Total	185 (100.0%)	119 (100.0%)	66 (100.0%)

Money is always an issue in any project, and software development projects are no exception. The purpose of question six was to assess the size of a project in terms of the dollars budgeted. The data contained in Table 10 is comprised of all projects, all known agile-driven plus probable agile-driven projects, and all known plan-driven plus probable plan-driven projects. As in the previous subsections, for discussion purposes the projects are congregated by size, where small-sized projects possessed budgets less than $250,000, medium-sized projects had budgets that ranged from $250,000 to $999,999, and large-sized projects enjoyed budgets of $1,000,000 or more.

Forty-four of the 185 total projects in the study had budgets less than $50,000, where 31 of these projects were known agile-driven or probable agile-driven, whereas the 13 remaining projects were known plan-driven or probable plan-driven. For the 29 projects with budgets between $50,000 and $99,999, 20 were known agile-driven plus probable agile-driven projects and nine were known plan-driven plus probable plan-driven projects. Of the 18 projects that possessed budgets ranging from $100,000 to $249,999, 11 projects were known agile-driven or probable agile-driven, and seven projects were known plan-driven or probable plan-driven. Thus, 62 of the 119 or 52.1% of all known agile-driven plus probable agile-driven projects could be classified as small-sized projects, and 29 of the 66 or 43.9% of all known plan-driven plus probable plan-driven projects could be construed to be small-sized projects.

There were 29 projects that had budgets between $250,000 and $499,999, where 21 of these projects were known agile-driven or probable agile-driven, and eight of the projects were known plan-driven or probable plan-driven. For the 21 projects that enjoyed budgets between $500,000 and $999,999, 12 projects were reported to be known agile-driven or probable agile-driven projects and nine projects were said to be known plan-driven or probable plan-driven projects. Assuming the project budget classification described above, 27.1% of all known agile-driven plus probable agile-driven projects were medium-sized projects, whereas 25.7% of all known plan-driven plus probable plan-driven projects were medium-sized projects. In terms for project budget size, no inferences seemed to be warranted for medium-sized projects.

From the 25 projects with budgets between $1,000,000 and $4,999,999, there were 15 known agile-driven plus probable agile-driven projects, and 10 known plan-driven plus probable plan-driven projects. Of the remaining 19 projects with budgets of $5,000,000 or more, nine of these projects turned up to be known agile-driven plus probable agile-driven projects, whereas 10 were registered as known plan-driven plus probable plan-driven projects. In other words, 20.2% of all known agile-driven plus probable agile-driven projects were large-sized projects and 30.4% of all known plan-driven plus probable plan-driven projects were large-sized projects. Thus, in terms of project budgets, the data seemed to indicate that the larger the project budget the greater the likelihood that any given project would employ plan-driven software development methods over agile-driven software development methods.

Duration of the Projects. The purpose of question seven in the survey was to inquire about the length of time that expired from the completion of a project to the actual time when the questionnaire was completed. The idea is that a participant's memory may have faded over time, and that negative impressions about a software development project would be ignored as the value of the software product superimposed itself on these negative memories. Furthermore, positive impressions could be enhanced with the passage of time, as the value of the software product built upon these positive memories. Furthermore, because agile-driven software development methodologies appeared in 2001, it was expected that there would be more recent known agile-driven plus probable agile-driven projects than known plan-driven plus probable plan-driven projects. Table 11 contains the responses to question seven, and the data appeared to confirm this expectation.

In Table 11, 43 projects were completed less than one month before the participant responded to the questionnaire, and 33 of the projects were known agile-driven or probable agile-driven, whereas 10 of the projects were known plan-driven or probable plan-driven. Furthermore, 41 projects finished between one and three months before a respondent answered the survey questions, where 33 projects were known agile-driven or probable agile-driven and 10 projects were known plan-driven or probable plan-driven. Third, 27 projects ended four to six months before the participant submitted their responses, where 18 projects were known agile-driven or probable agile-driven, and nine projects were known plan-driven or probable plan-driven. In total, 111 or 60.0% of all of the projects in the study were completed six or less months prior to the participant responding to the questionnaire. Of these 111 projects, 82 projects were known agile-driven or probable agile-driven, and 29 projects were known plan-driven or probable plan driven. In other words, a supermajority of the known agile-driven plus probable agile-driven projects were finished six or less months prior to the participant answering the questions of the survey. Less than a simple majority of the known plan-driven plus probable plan-driven projects were completed in six or less months prior to the respondent providing his or her data for this study.

Table 11 *How Long Ago Was the Project Completed?*

How Long Ago Was the Project Completed	All Projects	Known Agile-Driven plus Probable Agile-Driven Projects	Known Plan-Driven plus Probable Plan-Driven Projects
	Count (Percent)	Count (Percent)	Count (Percent)
Less than 1 month ago	43 (23.2%)	33 (27.7%)	10 (15.2%)
1 - 3	41 (22.2%)	31 (26.1%)	10 (15.2%)
4 - 6	27 (14.6%)	18 (15.1%)	9 (13.6%)
7 - 9	17 (9.2%)	11 (9.2%)	6 (9.1%)
10 - 12	16 (8.6%)	9 (7.6%)	7 (10.5%)
13 - 18	14 (7.6%)	8 (6.7%)	6 (9.1%)
Over 18 months ago	27 (14.6%)	9 (7.6%)	18 (27.3%)
Total	185 (100.0%)	119 (100.0%)	66 (100.0%)

Forty-seven or 25.4% of the total projects occurred seven to 18 months prior to the questionnaire being completed, where 28 projects were known agile-driven or probable agile-driven, and 19 projects were known plan-driven or probable plan-driven. Finally, 27 projects were concluded over 18 months prior to the participant taking the survey, where nine of the projects were known agile-driven or probable agile-driven, and 18 of the projects were known plan-driven or probable plan-driven. This last statement was significant because only 7.6% of the known agile-driven plus probable agile-driven software development projects ended more than 18 months before the data were collected from a participant. In contrast, 27.3% of the known plan-driven or probable plan-driven projects enjoyed this same characteristic. This result was expected because plan-driven software development methodologies are approximately 10 to 20 years older than agile-driven methods.

Another tenet of the agile software development community is that agile-driven methods work well in a project of short duration (Highsmith, 2004; Schwaber, 2004). Question eight of the survey in Appendix C endeavored to verify the estimated durations of agile-driven and plan-driven projects. The idea is that small-sized projects are of a short duration, medium-sized projects are of a moderate duration, and large-sized projects are of a lengthy duration. For the purposes of discussion, it is posited that projects of short estimated duration were six or less months in length, projects of moderate estimated duration were between six and 12 months long, and projects of a lengthy estimated duration were 13 or more months long.

Table 12 portrays the raw estimated project duration data gathered in this study. Thirty-three projects were estimated to take less than three months to complete, where 25 projects were known agile-driven or probable agile-driven, and eight projects were known plan-driven or probable plan-driven. Furthermore, the estimated duration of 52 projects was between four and six months long, where 32 projects were known agile-driven or probable agile-driven, and 20 projects were known plan-driven or probable plan-driven. Thus, 85 of all of the projects were estimated to be of a short duration, where 57 projects were known agile-driven or probable agile-driven, and 28 projects were known plan-driven or probable plan-driven. From this data, it appeared that there was not a significant difference in the estimated project durations between agile-driven projects and plan-driven projects.

Table 12 *Estimated Project Durations*

Estimated Project Durations	All Projects	Known Agile-Driven plus Probable Agile-Driven Projects	Known Plan-Driven plus Probable Plan-Driven Projects
	Count (Percent)	Count (Percent)	Count (Percent)
Under 3 months	33 (17.8%)	25 (21.0%)	8 (12.1%)
4 - 6	52 (28.2%)	32 (27.0%)	20 (30.3%)
7 - 9	28 (15.1%)	22 (18.5%)	6 (9.1%)
10 – 12	31 (16.8%)	20 (16.8%)	11 (16.7%)
13 - 18	18 (9.7%)	6 (5.0%)	12 (18.2%)
19 - 24	10 (5.4%)	6 (5.0%)	4 (6.0%)
Over 24 months	13 (7.0%)	8 (6.7%)	5 (7.6%)
Total	185 (100.0%)	119 (100.0%)	66 (100.0%)

Assuming that moderate length software development projects were between seven and 12 months long, there were 28 projects that were estimated to last between seven and nine months, of which 22 projects were known agile-driven or probable agile-driven, and 6 projects were known plan-driven or probable plan-driven. Of the 31 projects that were estimated to last between 10 to 12 months, 20 projects were known agile-driven or probable agile-driven and 11 projects were known plan-driven or probable plan-driven. Thus, 35.3% of all known agile-driven plus probable agile-driven projects were estimated to be moderately long, whereas 25.8% of known plan-driven plus probable plan-driven projects shared this same classification. When projects of short and moderate estimated duration are grouped together, 81.3% of all known agile-driven plus probable agile-driven projects and 68.2% of all known plan-driven plus probable plan-driven projects were estimated to be 12 or fewer months in length. Thus, it seemed that the study indicated that in terms of estimated project duration, known agile-driven plus probable agile-driven software development projects were more common than known plan-driven plus probable plan-driven software development projects.

Finally, projects of estimated lengthy duration are discussed. For the 41 software development projects that were estimated to take 13 months or longer to complete, 20 projects were known agile-driven or probable agile-driven, and 21 projects were known plan-driven or probable plan-driven. In terms of percentages, 16.7% of all known agile-driven plus probable agile-driven projects were estimated to extend 13 or more months in length, whereas 31.8% of all known plan-driven plus probable plan-driven projects completed 13 or more months. This result appeared to show that when the estimated duration of a project was more than a year in length, plan-driven software development projects were more common than agile-driven software development projects.

The last step in understanding the characteristics of the projects contained in this study was to examine the actual project durations. Question nine of the survey in Appendix C tried to assess the actual durations of agile-driven and plan-driven projects. As assumed in the previous subsection, projects of short actual duration are six or less months in length, projects of moderate actual duration are between six and 12 months long, and projects of a lengthy actual duration are 13 or more months long.

Table 13 highlights the raw actual project duration data that were collected in this study. There were 27 projects with an actual duration less than three months, where 21 projects were known agile-driven or probable agile-driven, and six projects were known plan-driven or probable plan-driven. Furthermore, 39 projects took between four and six months to complete, where 27 projects were known agile-driven or probable agile-driven and 12 projects were known plan driven or probable plan-driven. In other words, 35.7% of all of the projects were of a short duration, 40.3% of all known agile-driven plus probable agile-driven projects were of a short duration, and 27.3% of all known plan-driven plus probable plan-driven projects were of a short duration.

Table 13 *Actual Project Durations*

Actual Project Durations	All Projects	Known Agile-Driven plus Probable Agile-Driven Projects	Known Plan-Driven plus Probable Plan-Driven Projects
	Count (Percent)	Count (Percent)	Count (Percent)
Under 3 months	27 (14.6%)	21 (17.6%)	6 (9.1%)
4 - 6	39 (21.1%)	27 (22.7%)	12 (18.2%)
7 - 9	30 (16.2%)	22 (18.5%)	8 (12.1%)
10 – 12	30 (16.2%)	19 (16.0%)	11 (16.7%)
13 - 18	28 (15.1%)	14 (11.8%)	14 (21.2%)
19 - 24	12 (6.5%)	5 (4.2%)	7 (10.6%)
Over 24 months	19 (10.3%)	11 (9.2%)	8 (12.1%)
Total	185 (100.0%)	119 (100.0%)	66 (100.0%)

The study contained 30 projects that lasted between seven and nine months in length, and 30 projects that were completed in 10 to 12 months. Of the known agile-driven plus probable agile-driven projects, 22 projects were between seven and nine months long, and 19 projects had actual durations between 10 and 12 months. For the known plan-driven plus probable plan-driven projects, eight projects finished in seven to nine months and 11 projects were done in 10 to 12 months. In other words, 32.4% of all of the projects, 34.5% of all of the known agile-driven plus probable agile-driven projects, and 28.8% of all known plan-driven plus probable plan-driven projects were of moderate length. In terms of actual duration, there did not appear to be a significant difference between known agile-driven plus probable agile-driven and known plan-driven plus probable plan-driven software development projects.

There were 59 software development projects that took more than a year to finish of which 30 projects were known agile-driven or probable agile-driven, and 29 projects were known plan-driven or probable plan-driven, where 25.2% of all known agile-driven plus probable agile-driven and 43.9% of all known plan-driven plus probable plan-driven projects lasted 13 months or more. In other words, in terms of percentages of the actual project duration, the data that were collected contained more plan-driven projects than agile-driven projects. This result was expected because the conventional wisdom states that plan-driven software development methodologies are quite prevalent in long and complex projects (Boehm & Turner, 2004).

Table 14 *All Projects - Means, Medians, and Standard Deviations of the Project Characteristics*

Project Characteristics	Count	Means	Medians	Standard Deviations
Number of Person Hours Expended	185	3,135 p.h.	2,603 p.h.	1,136 p.h.
Number of Project Team Members	185	11.0 ind.	6.4 ind.	6.5 ind.
Budgeted Dollar Amounts	185	$185,140	$167,020	$53,433
How Long Ago Was the Project Completed	185	5.2 mos.	3.6 mos.	1.3 mos.
Estimated Project Durations	185	7.5 mos.	6.5 mos.	2.3 mos.
Actual Project Durations	185	8.7 mos.	8.1 mos.	2.6 mos.

Note. The medians were calculated from grouped data.
Note. The abbreviations "p.h." stands for "person hours", "ind." denotes "individuals", and "mos." represents "months".

Means, Medians, and Standard Deviations. Because a 7-point Likert-type scale was used to capture the characteristics of the projects, it did not make sense to present the means, medians, and standard deviations as Likert-type decimal values. It is more meaningful to convert these statistics into results using the units of measure for each one of the six project characteristics. For example, if the mean number of person hours expended for all projects in this study was 3.5676 expressed using a 7-point Likert-type scale, it is more meaningful if this average value was expressed as 3,135 person hours. Thus, for all of the projects, Table 14 contains the means, medians and standard deviations for the six project characteristics using the appropriate units of measure.

From Table 14, the mean number of person hours expended in a project was 3,135 person hours, where the median was 2,603 person hours and a standard deviation of 1,136 person hours. The average number of project team members was 11.0 with a median of 6.4 individuals and a standard deviation of 6.5 persons. The mean budgeted dollar amount was $185,140, the median budgeted dollar amount was $167,020, and the standard deviation budgeted dollar amount was $53, 433. The average software development project was completed in 5.2 months prior to the participant taking the survey. The median time when the project ended was 3.6 months, and the standard deviation was 1.3 months. The mean estimated project duration was 7.5 months, and the average actual project duration was 8.7 months. The median estimated project duration was 6.5 months and the median actual project duration was 8.1 months. Finally, the standard deviation for the estimated project duration was 2.3 months and the standard deviation for the actual project duration was 2.6 months.

Table 15 *Known Agile-Driven plus Probable Agile-Driven Projects - Means, Medians, and Standard Deviations of the Project Characteristics*

Project Characteristics	Count	Means	Medians	Standard Deviations
Number of Person Hours Expended	119	2,303 p.h.	1,737 p.h.	1,032 p.h.
Number of Project Team Members	119	7.9 ind.	5.1 ind.	2.6 ind.
Budgeted Dollar Amounts	119	$155,455	$128,125	$50,395
How Long Ago Was the Project Completed	119	3.8 mos.	2.3 mos.	.9 mos.
Estimated Project Durations	119	7.0 mos.	6.1 mos.	2.2 mos.
Actual Project Durations	119	7.9 mos.	7.1 mos.	2.5 mos.

Note. The medians were calculated from grouped data.
Note. The abbreviations "p.h." stands for "person hours", "ind." denotes "individuals", and "mos." represents "months".

When examining Table 15, the average number of person hours expended in known agile-driven plus probable agile-driven projects was 2,303 person hours. The median number of person hours expended was 1,737 person hours, and the standard deviation was 1,032 person hours. Another interesting characteristic of the known agile-driven plus probable agile-driven projects was that the mean number of project team members was 7.9 individuals, 3.1 individuals less than when all 185 software development projects were combined. The median number of project team members was 5.1 with a standard deviation of 2.6 individuals. The average budgeted dollar amount for known agile-driven plus probable agile-driven projects was $155,455, down by $29,685 for all of the projects in the study. The median budgeted dollar amount was $128,125 and the standard deviation was $50,395. In other words, the agile software development projects in the study were small projects in terms of the amount of money spent to accomplish them. The projects highlighted in Table 15 occurred on the average 3.8 months from the time that the participant submitted his or her data collected by the questionnaire. The median time was 2.3 months and the standard deviation was .9 months. The mean estimated project duration for known agile-driven plus probable agile-driven projects was 7.0 months, where the median estimated project duration was 6.1 months and the standard deviation was 2.2 months. The average actual duration of a known agile-driven plus probable agile-driven software development project was 7.9 months, less than one month greater than its estimated counterpart. The median actual duration was 7.1 months and the standard deviation was 2.5 months. From Table 16, it is apparent that the actual average, median and standard deviation for known agile-driven plus probable agile-driven projects slightly exceed the estimated average, median, and standard deviation.

Table 16 *Known Plan-Driven plus Probable Plan-Driven Projects - Means, Medians, and Standard Deviations of the Project Characteristics*

Project Characteristics	Count	Means	Medians	Standard Deviations
Number of Person Hours Expended	66	5,273 p.h.	5,556 p.h.	1,127 p.h.
Number of Project Team Members	66	16.7 ind.	9.1 ind.	10.9 ind.
Budgeted Dollar Amounts	66	$238,630	$250,000	$57,170
How Long Ago Was the Project Completed	66	7.6 mos.	7.5 mos.	1.7 mos.
Estimated Project Durations	66	8.4 mos.	7.7 mos.	2.4 mos.
Actual Project Durations	66	7.1 mos.	7.4 mos.	2.6 mos.

Note. The medians were calculated from grouped data.
Note. The abbreviations "p.h." stands for "person hours", "ind." denotes "individuals", and "mos." represents "months".

Table 16 is similar to Table 15, but contains the means, medians, and standard deviations for known plan-driven plus probable plan-driven projects. The mean number of known plan-driven plus probable plan-driven projects was 5,273 person hours, more twice the average number of person hours expended for known agile-driven plus probable agile-driven projects. The median number of person hours expended was 5,556 person hours with a standard deviation of 1,127 person hours. Please note that the median number of person hours expended was more than three times the median value for known agile-driven plus probable agile-driven projects. The number of project team members for known plan-driven plus probable plan-driven projects was 16.7 individuals, where the median was 9.1 team members with a standard deviation of 10.9 individuals. This apparently significant increase of human resources could be attributed to the intensity of documentation that is required by plan-driven software development methods, and will be discussed in the analysis of the findings section of this chapter.

The average budgeted dollar amount for known plan-driven plus probable plan-driven projects was $238, 630, an increase of $83,175 for known agile-driven plus probable agile-driven projects. The median budgeted dollar amount was $250,000 and the standard deviation was $57,170. Note that the median budgeted dollar amount for known plan-driven plus probable plan-driven projects was slightly under twice the median for known agile-driven plus probable agile-driven projects, and that the two standard deviations are approximately the same value. From Table 16, known plan-driven plus probable plan-driven projects were completed on the average 7.6 months before the participant submitted his or her data, approximately twice the length of time for known agile-driven plus probable agile-driven projects. The median length of time was 7.5 months and the standard deviation was 1.7 months.

The mean estimated duration of a known plan-driven plus probable plan-driven project was 8.4 months, whereas the median estimated duration was 7.7 months with a standard deviation of 2.4 months. The mean actual duration was 7.1 months, or 1.3 months less than the average estimated duration. The median actual duration was 7.4 months, or 0.3 months smaller than the estimated median. The standard deviation for the actual duration of a known plan-driven plus probable plan-driven project was 2.6 months, or .2 months greater than the standard deviation for the estimated duration of a known plan-driven plus probable plan-driven software development projects.

Characteristics of the Participants

In the survey contained in Appendix C, questions 46 through 50 attempted to characterize the participants. The questions dealt with the occupation of a participant, the number of years that a participant was engaged in his or her present occupation, the major role that a participant played in the project under consideration, the approximate age of a participant, and the gender of a participant. Question 46 contained 40 occupations based on the Bureau of Labor Statistics with the opportunity for a participant to enter an occupation not included in the list (Bureau of Labor Statistics, 2008). Question 47 dealt with the number of years that a person was engaged in the stated occupation, and consisted of six distinct groups. The possible responses to question 48 were suggested by the Project Management Institute (PMBOK Guide, 2005). Question 49 was made up of seven age groups. Finally, the responses to question 50 were male or female.

Table 17 *Occupational Classification*

Occupational Classifications	All Projects	Known Agile-Driven plus Probable Agile-Driven Projects	Known Plan-Driven plus Probable Plan-Driven Projects
	Count (Percent)	Count (Percent)	Count (Percent)
Business and Financial Operations	16 (8.6%)	9 (7.6%)	7 (10.6%)
Computer and Mathematical	63 (34.1%)	46 (38.7%)	17 (25.8%)
Education, Training, Library, and Museums	10 (5.4%)	5 (4.1%)	5 (7.6%)
Middle-Level Management	34 (18.4%)	22 (18.5%)	12 (18.2%)
Senior-Level Management	22 (11.9%)	14 (11.8%)	8 (12.1%)
Miscellaneous	27 (14.6%)	14 (11.8%)	13 (19.7%)
Other	13 (7.0%)	9 (7.5%)	4 (6.0%)
Total	185 (100.0%)	119 (100.0%)	66 (100.0%)

Work Related Issues. In presenting the occupations of the participants in Table 17, there were five major occupations; namely, business and financial operations, computer and mathematical occupations, education, training, library, and museum occupations, middle-level management occupations, and senior-level management occupations. A number of occupations of various participants are reported in this dissertation as miscellaneous occupations. Finally, 13 participants engaged in occupations that were not listed in the pre-defined responses to question 46.

Sixteen participants stated that his or her occupation was in business and financial operations, where nine participants were reporting on known agile-driven plus probable agile-driven projects, and seven participants provided data on known plan-driven plus probable plan-driven projects. Furthermore, 63 participants were employed in computer and mathematical occupations, where 46 participants supplied data on projects that used or probably used agile-driven methods and 17 participants gave data on plan-driven projects. There were 10 participants in education, training, library, or museum occupations with five respondents contributing data on agile software development projects and five respondents using plan-driven software development methods.

Of the 34 participants who classified themselves as middle-level managers, 22 respondents reported on known agile-driven plus probable agile-driven projects, and 12 respondents provided data on known plan-driven plus probable plan-driven projects. Twenty-two participants were senior managers, whereas 14 respondents supplied data on projects using or probably using agile-driven methods, and eight respondents contributed data on known plan-driven plus probable plan-driven projects. Twenty-seven participants made up the various miscellaneous occupations, with 14 respondents associated with projects using agile-driven methodologies and 13 respondents affiliated with projects employing plan-driven methodologies. Finally, there were 13 participants who stated that their occupation that it was other than one of the 40 occupations listed in the question, where nine respondents reported data on known agile-driven plus probable agile-driven projects and four respondents giving data on known plan-driven plus probable plan-driven projects.

Table 18 *Years in the Selected Occupation*

Years in the Selected Occupation	All Projects	Known Agile-Driven plus Probable Agile-Driven Projects	Known Plan-Driven plus Probable Plan-Driven Projects
	Count (Percent)	Count (Percent)	Count (Percent)
1 – 11 months	3 (1.6%)	3 (2.5%)	0 (0.0%)
1 – 2 years	11 (5.9%)	8 (6.7%)	3 (4.5%)
3 - 5	32 (17.3%)	19 (16.0%)	13 (19.7%)
6 - 10	47 (25.4%)	28 (23.5%)	19 (28.9%)
11 - 20	44 (23.8%)	29 (24.4%)	15 (22.7%)
Over 20 years	48 (26.0%)	32 (26.9%)	16 (24.2%)
Total	185 (100.0%)	119 (100.0%)	66 (100.0%)

Table 18 contains the numbers of participants who engaged in the occupations selected in question 47 of the survey for a specified number of years. There were three participants who worked in their selected occupation for less than one year, all of whom were associated with known agile-driven plus probable agile-driven projects. Of the 11 respondents who worked between one and two years in their chosen occupation, eight were allied with software development projects using agile or probable agile-driven methods and three were connected to software development projects employing known plan-driven plus probable plan-driven methods.

The next four categories for this question contained the vast majority of the participants. Thirty-two participants were engaged in his or her selected occupation for between three and five years, and 47 respondents divulged that he or she had the same career for between six and 10 years. Furthermore, 44 participants were engaged in his or her chosen profession for between 11 and 20 years, and 48 respondents revealed that he or she had been employed in the same line of work for over 20 years.

When the numbers in Table 18 are broken out between known agile plus probable agile-driven methods and known plan-driven plus probable plan-driven methods, what emerges is a similar picture. For participants that were engaged in his or her chosen profession for between three and five years, 19 or 16.0% worked on known agile-driven plus probable agile-driven projects and 13 or 19.7% were employed in known plan-driven plus probable plan-driven projects. When the interval increased to six to 10 years, 28 or 23.5% of the participants reported on known agile-driven plus probable agile-driven projects and 19 or 28.9% gave data on known plan-driven plus probable plan-driven projects. Furthermore, 29 or 23.4% of the respondents provided details on known agile-driven plus probable agile-driven projects, whereas 15 or 22.7% of the respondents conveyed data on known plan-driven plus probable plan-driven projects. Finally, 32 or 26.9% of the participants described the features of agile-driven or probable plan-driven projects, but 16 or 24.2% of the participants offered data on known plan-driven plus probable plan-driven projects. Thus, it is evident that in terms of the number of years that an individual worked in his or her selected occupation, the data were more or less homogeneous.

The possible options that the survey listed in question 48 came from the Project Management Institute (PMBOK Guide, 2005). The inventory of roles encompassed all of the functions that could arise during the execution of a project, regardless of what particular software development methodology was employed. The idea is that each individual would have a degree of understanding regarding the satisfaction experienced by customers. In particular, both agile-driven and plan-driven methods state that goal of the methodologies was to satisfy customers (Highsmith, 2004; Schwaber, 2004; Humphrey, 1999; Paulk et al.,

1994). Thus, it made sense to include the data from all possible team members, regardless of the role that he or she played in a project.

Although the data in Table 19 contains the details for each project role, for the purposes of this discussion the data could be combined into three categories. The first group consists of customers, users, customer decision makers, and customer representatives, and is called the "customers". The second class of participants are individuals are made up of steering committee members, executive sponsors, influencers, project sponsors, and project directors, and are denoted by the term "senior project managers". The third category consists of project managers, project team managers, and project team members, and is identified as "project team members".

Table 19 *Major Role Played*

Major Role Played	All Projects	Known Agile-Driven plus Probable Agile-Driven Projects	Known Plan-Driven plus Probable Plan-Driven Projects
	Count (Percent)	Count (Percent)	Count (Percent)
Customers or Users	6 (3.2%)	3 (2.5%)	3 (4.5%)
Customer Decision Makers	10 (5.4%)	4 (3.4%)	6 (9.1%)
Customer Representatives	3 (1.6%)	2 (1.7%)	1 (1.5%)
Steering Committee Members	7 (3.8%)	5 (4.2%)	2 (3.0%)
Executive Sponsors	5 (2.7%)	4 (3.4%)	1 (1.5%)
Influencers	11 (5.9%)	4 (3.4%)	7 (10.6%)
Project Sponsors	1 (0.5%)	0 (0.0%)	1 (1.5%)
Project Directors	34 (18.4%)	25 (21.0%)	9 (13.6%)
Project Managers	45 (24.4%)	28 (23.4%)	17 (25.9%)
Project Team Managers	27 (14.6%)	19 (16.0%)	8 (12.1%)
Project Team Members	36 (19.5%)	25 (21.0%)	11 (16.7%)
Total	185 (100.0%)	119 (100.0%)	66 (100.0%)

Table19 contains 19 participants who classified themselves as customers, where nine or 7.6% reported on known agile-driven plus probable agile-driven projects and 10 or 15.1% provided data on known plan-driven plus probable plan-driven projects. In other words, more than twice as many respondents who gave data on known plan-driven plus probable plan-driven projects than saw themselves as customers when compared to the respondents who furnished data on known agile-driven plus probable agile-driven projects. Of the 58 or 31.3% of the participants who could be classified as senior project managers, 38 or 32.0% dealt with known agile-driven plus probable agile-driven projects, whereas 20 or 30.2% presented data on known plan-driven plus probable plan-driven projects. From a percentage perspective, the two groups were almost the same size. Finally, 108 or 58.5% of the respondents could be groups together as project team members. Of these individuals, 72 or 60.5% were involved in known agile-driven plus probable agile-driven projects, and 36 or 54.7% worked on known plan-driven plus probable plan-driven projects.

Table 20 *Approximate Age*

Approximate Age	All Projects	Known Agile-Driven plus Probable Agile-Driven Projects	Known Plan-Driven plus Probable Plan-Driven Projects
	Count (Percent)	Count (Percent)	Count (Percent)
18 - 24 years	6 (3.2%)	5 (4.2%)	1 (1.5%)
25 - 30	30 (16.2%)	22 (18.5%)	8 (12.1%)
31 - 39	63 (34.1%)	38 (31.9%)	25 (37.9%)
40 - 49	47 (25.4%)	30 (25.2%)	17 (25.8%)
50 - 59	29 (15.7%)	20 (16.8%)	9 (13.6%)
60 - 65	8 (4.3%)	4 (3.4%)	4 (6.1%)
Over 65 years	2 (1.1%)	0 (0.0%)	2 (3.0%)
Total	185 (100.0%)	119 (100.0%)	66 (100.0%)

Personal Issues. Because plan-driven software development methods are 10 to 20 years older than agile-driven methods, it was reasonable to expect that the participants associated with known plan-driven plus probable plan-driven software development technologies were chronologically older than his or her agile-driven counterparts. However, the data in Table 20 indicated that the populations were somewhat homogeneous when it came to age.

For the six individuals between the ages of 18 and 24 years old, five of the participants engaged in known agile-driven plus probable agile-driven projects, and only one participant reported on a known plan-driven plus probable plan-driven projects. There were 30 participants between the ages of 25 and 30 years old, and 22 were involved in known agile-driven plus probable agile-driven projects and eight provided data on known plan-driven plus probable plan-driven projects. Of the 63 people who said that they were between 31 and 39 years old, 38 gave data on known agile-driven plus probable agile-driven projects, and 25 provided data on known plan-driven plus probable plan-driven projects. Of the 185 total participants in the study, 99 were aged 39 years or younger and comprised 53.5% of the respondents. Of these 99 individuals, 65 of the participants described known agile-driven plus probable agile-driven projects, and 34 of the respondents told about known plan-driven plus probable plan-driven projects. In other words, of the people who provided data on known agile-driven plus probable agile-driven projects, 54.6% of these individuals were 39 years old or younger, and of the people who reported known plan-driven plus probable plan-driven projects, 51.5% of these participants were less than 40 years old. Thus, it was apparent that for both software development methodologies, the two percentages were approximately equal.

Table 21 *Gender*

Gender	All Projects	Known Agile-Driven plus Probable Agile-Driven Projects	Known Plan-Driven plus Probable Plan-Driven Projects
	Count (Percent)	Count (Percent)	Count (Percent)
Male	155 (83.8%)	99 (83.2%)	56 (84.8%)
Female	30 (16.2%)	20 (16.8%)	10 (15.2%)
Total	185 (100.0%)	119 (100.0%)	66 (100.0%)

Eighty-six individuals responded to the questionnaire in Appendix C and were 40 or more years old. These people comprised 46.5% of the participants. Of these 86 people, 54 supplied data on known agile-driven plus probable agile-driven projects, and 32 furnished data on known plan-driven plus probable plan-driven projects. In other words, 45.4% of the individuals who reported on known agile-driven plus probable agile-driven projects were at

least 40 years of age, whereas 48.5% of the people who described known plan-driven plus
probable plan-driven projects were 40 years old or more. Thus, based on age, it was evident
that the two populations contained approximately the same percentage of participants.

Table 21 presents the gender of the respondents who participated in the study. Of the
185 total respondents, 155 were male and 30 were female. In other words, 83.8% of all the
participants were male and 16.2% were female. For known agile-driven plus probable agile-
driven projects, 99 or 83.2% of the participants were male and 20 or 16.8% of the
respondents were female. As for the known plan-driven plus probable plan-driven projects,
56 or 84.8% of the participants were male and 10 or 15.2% of the respondents were female.
Thus, the data in Table 21 shows that there no gender-based disparities for the participants.

Table 22 *Means, Medians, and Standard Deviations of the Participant Characteristics*

Participant Characteristics	Count	Means	Medians	Standard Deviations
All Projects				
Years in Selected Occupation	185	8.1 yrs.	8.5 yrs.	.3 yrs.
Approximate Age	185	35.6 yrs.	35.1 yrs.	1.5 yrs.
Known Agile-Driven plus Probable Agile-Driven Projects				
Years in Selected Occupation	119	8.1 yrs.	8.7 yrs.	.3 yrs.
Approximate Age	119	34.8 yrs.	34.6 yrs	1.3 yrs.
Known Plan-Driven plus Probable Plan-Driven Projects				
Years in Selected Occupation	66	8.1 yrs.	8.2 yrs	.2 yrs.
Approximate Age	66	37.1 yrs.	35.9 yrs.	1.8 yrs.

Note. The medians were calculated from grouped data. Furthermore, "yrs." stands for "years".

Means, Medians, and Standard Deviations. Even though questions 46 through 50 in
the questionnaire used 5-point Likert-type responses, only questions 47 and 49 had
underlying continuous units of measure. Thus, in discussing the means, medians, and
standard deviations of the characteristics of the participants, it only makes sense to talk about
the mean, medians, and standard deviations for the number of years that a participant was
engaged in his or her selected occupation and the age of the respondent. Since both questions
47 and 49 employed 6-point and 7-point Likert-type scales respectively, the mean, medians,

and standard deviations were converted into statistics that make sense using the units of measure for each question. Table 22 contains the results.

For all 185 participants, the average number of years in a respondent's selected occupation was 8.1 years, where the median was 85.years and the standard deviation was .3 years. The mean age of all of the individuals who took the survey was 35.6 years, with a median age of 35.1 years and a standard deviation of 1.5 years. Of the 119 participants who reported on known agile-driven plus probable agile-driven projects, the mean number of years in his or her chosen profession was also 8.1 years with a median value of 8.7 years and a standard deviation of .3 years. For this same population, the mean age was 34.8 years where the median age was 34.6 years with a standard deviation of 1.3 years. Finally, for the 66 respondents who gave data on known plan-driven plus probable plan-driven projects, the number of years that a participant was engaged in his or her selected occupation was 8.1 years for the third time with a median value of 8.2 years and a standard deviation of .2 years. The mean age was 37.1 years with median value of 35.9 years and a standard deviation of 1.8 years. In terms of the years of experience in his or her selected occupation, agile-driven and plan-driven populations appear to be about the same, whereas in terms of age, the plan-driven population is on the average 2.3 years older than the agile-driven population. Again, in terms of the age of the participants, the two populations appeared on the surface to be more or less the same.

Potential Problems with a Project

Question 42 of the survey attempted to discover the most significant problem that was encountered during the course of a project. Of the 17 listed possibilities, 12 responses dealt with the behavior of the project team, two responses were concerned with the features, of the project, and one response addressed the behavior of the project manager. The questionnaire provided a participant an opportunity to enter a significant problem not listed in the pre-specified responses. If a respondent selected the last option, then he or she indicated that no significant problems were encountered while the project was executing. Table 23 contains the results obtained from the participants. Only the more common problems are listed in the table, and a number of the responses are combined into a miscellaneous category.

Table 23 *Most Significant Problems Encountered*

Most Significant Problems Encountered	All Projects	Known Agile-Driven plus Probable Agile-Driven Projects	Known Plan-Driven plus Probable Plan-Driven Projects
	Count (Percent)	Count (Percent)	Count (Percent)
Lacked Knowledge of Products & Services	15 (8.1%)	6 (5.0%)	9 (13 .6%)
Did not Do What Was Said Would Be Done	5 (2.7%)	3 (2.5%)	2 (3.0%)
Attitude not Positive	6 (3.2%)	5 (4.2%)	1 (1.5%)
Specifications not Clearly Understood	25 (13.5%)	18 (15.1%)	7 (10.6%)
Reasonable Explanations not Provided	5 (2.7%)	5 (4.2%)	0 (0.0%)
Miscellaneous Problems	24 (13.0%)	15 (12.6%)	9 (13.6%)
Other Significant Problems	32 (17.3%)	21 (17.6%)	11 (16.7%)
No Significant Problems	73 (39.5%)	46 (38.8%)	27 (41.0%)
Total	185 (100.0%)	119 (100.0%)	66 (100.0%)

For all 185 projects, 15 or 8.1% of the respondents indicated that the project team lacked knowledge of the products and services offered by the company. Five or 2.7% of the participants stated that the project team did not do what they said would be done, and six or 3.2% of the participants complained that the attitude of the project team was not positive. Twenty-five or 13.5% of the respondents believed that the project specifications were not clearly understood by the project team. Furthermore, 24 or 13.0% of the participants selected miscellaneous but significant problems encountered during the course of the project, and 32 or 17.3% of the participants stated that the project ran into an issue not listed in the set of pre-specified responses. Finally, 73 or 39.5% of the respondents affirmed that no significant problems were encountered.

For the known agile-driven plus probable agile-driven projects, six or 5.0% of the participants indicated that the project team lacked knowledge of company products and services. In contrast, nine or 13.6% of the respondents that reported on known plan-driven plus probable plan-driven projects believed that the project team was uninformed regarding the organization's products and services. Furthermore, for known agile-driven plus probable agile-driven projects, three or 2.5% of the participants observed that the project team did not do what was said would be done, whereas two or 3.0% of the participants who provided data on known plan-driven plus probable plan-driven projects believed that the project team said one thing and did something else. Five or 4.2% of the respondents that were involved in known agile-driven plus probable agile-driven projects stated that the attitude of the project team was not positive, whereas only one respondent that was associated with known plan-driven plus probable plan-driven projects felt the same way.

For the pre-defined options in question 42, the most common response of the participants was that the project team did not clearly understand the project specifications. Eighteen or 15.1% of the respondents who reported on known agile-driven plus probable agile-driven projects believed that the project team did not understand the project specifications, whereas only seven or 10.6% of the respondents who were associated with known plan-driven plus probable plan-driven projects gave the same answer. This result could exist because agile-driven methods are less concerned with project documentation than plan-driven methods, where project documentation is an emphasized feature of these software development methodologies. Furthermore, five or 4.2% of the participants who provided data on known agile-driven plus probable agile-driven projects thought that the project team did not provide reasonable explanations when decisions were made. In contrast, none of the participants that were connected with known plan-driven plus probable plan-driven projects gave the same response.

Twenty-one or 17.6% of the participants associated with known agile-driven plus probable agile-driven projects provided his or her own most significant problem, and are included in Table 23. It is interesting that some of the participants believed that agile software development methods were difficult to implement or that the project team was all too willing to embrace the methodology. Several respondents stated that there was a lack of customer involvement in the agile-driven project, not enough stories were written, not enough testing was done, and on one occasion, the software application broke when in production. The fact that two respondents stated that the specifications were not clearly stated and that the requirements were not well-defined is indicative that the agile philosophy was not clearly understood by the project team. Scope creep, working in different time zone, and too many dynamic interfaces are all issues that are independent of the software development methodology employed.

Table 24 *Other Significant Problems Encountered in Known Agile-Driven plus Probable Agile-Driven Projects*

Other Significant Problems Encountered
Project was delayed due to an undiscovered dependency.
The agile-driven method used was a new process and difficult to implement.
The customer was marginally involved in the project.
No one reported that the program broke when it was in production.
Not enough testing was done.
Other business processes could not keep up with Scrum.
Product owners did not write enough stories.
The project team struggled with the Agile/Scrum philosophy.
The requirements were not nailed down in a timely manner.
The project team resisted working in a collaborative manner.
Scope creep existed during the course of the project.
A technical direction change occurred during the project life cycle.
The customer kept changing his or her mind on what were the requirements.
The customer was not responsive to the requests of the project team.
The project specifications were not clearly stated.
The project requirements were not well-defined.
There were too many dynamic interfaces in the software application.
The project team worked in different time zones.
The XP project team was too willing to embrace change.

Furthermore, 11 or 16.7% of the participants who were involved in known plan-driven plus probable plan-driven projects provided his or her own most significant problem, and are reported in Table 25. In contrast to the problems listed in Table 24, a number of the issues raised in Table 25 are technical in nature. Data security, integration problems, technical issues, double-byte character representations, and the number of bugs found are all issues that can occur in any project, regardless of the software development methodology employed. Furthermore, there were four concerns raised about the behavior of the project team. Language barriers, corporate technology, insufficient customer involvement, the desire to go onto the next project, and understanding the level of effort needed to complete a project in a timely manner are again all issues that a project team can face, but are not necessarily related to the plan-driven software development methodology used. Finally, there was only one concern that dealt directly with the use of a plan-driven methodology; namely, the lack of realistic detailed planning. The apparent lack of concern with the software development methodology employed seems to be important, because it could be construed that plan-driven methodologies were well understood by the participants.

Table 25 *Other Significant Problems Encountered in Known Plan-Driven plus Probable Plan-Driven Projects*

Other Significant Problems Encountered
Some small to medium companies demanded there be no risk in handling and reporting their data. This is impossible to achieve.
There was insufficient cooperation with the client.
Integration problems occurred with other software factory systems.
There was a lack of realistic detailed planning.
A language barrier existed among the team members.
The project team was hindered by the corporate technology and by senior management issues.
Technical issues were difficult to resolve.
There were software issues regarding the support of double-byte characters.
The integration of the software ran too long due to the number of bugs found.
At the end of the project, the project team was too eager to move onto another software development project, and did not want to fix existing bugs.
The project team did not understand the amount of effort that was needed to complete the project.

Finally, from Table 23, 73 or 39.5% of all the participants encountered no significant problems, where 46 of these respondents were associated with known agile-driven plus probable agile-driven projects and 27 of these respondents were involved in known plan-driven plus probable plan-driven projects. From a percentage perspective, 38.8% of the participants that were engaged in known agile-driven plus probable agile-driven projects encountered no significant problems, and 41.0% of the participants that were involved with known plan-driven plus probable plan-driven projects also experienced no significant problems. Thus, it appears that these two percentages are approximately the same.

Regression Findings

In this section of the findings chapter, the results of four regressions are presented. The first regression included 148 data points, or the known agile-driven and known plan-driven projects. The dependent variable was customer satisfaction, and the independent variables were product quality, project team effectiveness, and project management effectiveness. A dummy variable was also included in the list of explanatory variables, where its value was zero for known plan-driven projects and one for known agile-driven projects. The purpose of the dummy variable was to capture the contribution that the use and results of employing agile-driven methods had on autonomous customer satisfaction. In this case, a participant explicitly stated that he or she knew that the software development methodology employed was either agile-driven or plan-driven. In other words, if a respondent selected the first or second options in question two, then that data were included in the first regression.

In the second regression, again the known agile-driven and known plan-driven projects were employed, but the dummy variable was no longer present in the regression equation because its coefficient was shown to be statistically insignificant at the 95% confidence level. The third regression contained all 185 data points and dummy variable that equaled zero for known plan-driven plus probable plan-driven projects and one for known agile-driven plus probable agile-driven projects. The fourth regression again used all 185 data points, but did not contain a dummy variable because its coefficient was not statistically significant at the 99% confidence level even though the coefficient was statistically significant at the 95% confidence level. The reason that the dummy variable was removed is because the dependent variable and the explanatory variables contained averaged values, and Brace and Brace-Pellillo (2009) as well as Bonferroni (1935, 1936) recommended employing a 99% confidence level instead of a 95% confidence level.

One issue that needs to be addressed is that it could be construed that the characteristics of the projects and/or the characteristics of the participants that were previously discussed should and ought to be in the regression equation because the values of these variables may affect customer satisfaction. Several regressions equations were estimated that included these variables to see if the non-standardized estimates of coefficients were statistically significant that either the 95% or 99% confidence levels. However, when these additional explanatory variables were included in the regression equation, only the non-standardized estimate of the coefficient for the estimated project duration was statistically significant at the 95% confidence level. When the regression equation contained the dummy variable, project quality, project team effectiveness, project management effectiveness, and the estimated project duration, the non-standardized estimate of the coefficient for the estimated project duration was statistically insignificant at the 95% confidence level, whereas the non-standardized estimates for the coefficients for the other explanatory variables were statistically significant at the 99% confidence level. Thus, it appeared that the initial statistical significance at the 95% confidence level of the non-standardized estimate of coefficient for the estimated project duration was a false positive, and could be attributed to chance as discussed by Bonferroni (1935, 1936). The implication is that for agile-driven and plan-driven projects, the appropriate explanatory variables appear indeed to be product quality, project team effectiveness, and project management effectiveness.

Table 26 *Means, Medians, and Standard Deviations for the Dependent and Explanatory Variables when the Software Development Methodology Is Known*

Known Agile-Driven and Known Plan-Driven Projects	Count	Means	Medians	Standard Deviations
Known Agile-Driven Projects				
Customer Satisfaction	95	4.000	4.190	.819
Product Quality	95	3.403	3.494	.683
Project Team Effectiveness	95	3.988	4.031	.653
Project Management Effectiveness	95	2.821	2.664	.766
Known Plan-Driven Projects				
Customer Satisfaction	53	3.551	3.725	1.044
Product Quality	53	3.137	3.143	.691
Project Team Effectiveness	53	3.767	3.764	.696
Project Management Effectiveness	53	2.976	2.900	.664

Known Software Development Methodologies. Before presenting the two regressions when the software development methodology was known, the means, medians, and the standard deviations for customer satisfaction, product quality, project team effectiveness, and project management effectiveness variables are shown in Table 26, where data are segregated in the table by whether the software development methodology was known to be agile-driven or known to be plan-driven. It is evident that the means and medians of customer satisfaction, product quality, project team effectiveness, and project management effectiveness for the agile-driven software development projects are larger than the corresponding means and medians for the plan-driven software development projects. Furthermore, the standard deviations of the model variables for known agile-driven projects are smaller than the standard deviations of the model variables for known plan-driven projects.

Table 27 *Model Summary Using the Known Agile-Driven Projects and Known Plan-Driven Projects with a Dummy Variable*

Explanatory Variables	R	R Square	Adjusted R Square	Std. Error of the Estimate
(Constant)	.825	.681	.672	.5313814
Dummy Variable				
Product Quality				
Project Team Effectiveness				
Project Management Effectiveness				

Note. Customer Satisfaction was the dependent variable.
Note. The Dummy Variable equaled zero for known plan-driven projects and one for known agile-driven projects.

In this first regression analysis, Table 27 encapsulates the results. The R-squared value was .681, suggesting that the constant term, the dummy variable, product quality, project team effectiveness, and project management effectiveness explained 68.1% of the variance in customer satisfaction for known agile-driven and known plan-driven projects. The adjusted R-squared value was .672, meaning that the model explained 67.2% of the variance in customer satisfaction, adjusted for the degrees of freedom. Because the actual R-squared value and the adjusted R-squared value was .009, this model is useful in estimating customer satisfaction when the software development methodology is known.

Table 28 *Analysis of Variance Statistics Using the Known Agile-Driven Projects and Known Plan-Driven Projects with a Dummy Variable*

Source of Variation	Sum of Squares	df	Mean Square	F	Sig.
Regression	86.314	4	21.579	76.421	.000
Residual	40.378	143	.282		
Total	126.693	147			

Note. Customer Satisfaction was the dependent variable.
Note. The explanatory variables were: (Constant), Dummy Variable, Product Quality, Project Team Effectiveness, and Project Management Effectiveness.
Note. The Dummy Variable equaled zero for known plan-driven projects and one for known agile-driven projects.

Table 28 contains the ANOVA statistics, and the value of $F(4,143)$ was 76.421, where the *p*-value was .000. The two statistics suggested that the model is again useful in estimating customer satisfaction for software development projects, and that there is a significant connection between customer satisfaction and product quality, project team effectiveness, and project management effectiveness.

Table 29 *Regression Results Using Known Agile-Driven Projects and Known Plan-Driven Projects with a Dummy Variable*

Explanatory Variables	Non-standardized Coefficients		Standardized Coefficients		
	B	Std. Error	Beta	t	Sig.
(Constant)	1.435	.499		2.875	.005
Dummy Variable	.172	.093	.089	1.852	.066
Product Quality	.443	.082	.332	5.388	.000
Project Team Effectiveness	.473	.087	.344	5.441	.000
Project Management Effectiveness	-.354	.076	-.280	-4.678	.000

Note. Customer Satisfaction was the dependent variable.
Note. The Dummy Variable equaled zero for known plan-driven projects and one for known agile-driven projects.

Table 29 records the results of the regression, including the non-standardized coefficients, the standardized coefficients, the values of the *t*-statistics, and the *p*-values. The estimated of the constant term, or autonomous customer satisfaction, was 1.435 with a standard error of .499, the value of the *t*-statistic was 2.875 and the *p*-value was .005. In other words, the constant term was significant at the 99% confidence level. For the dummy variable, the estimated value of the coefficient was .172 with a standard error or .093, the β-value was .089, the t-statistic was 1.854, and the p-value was .066. This means that the non-standardized coefficient of the dummy variable was not statistically significant at the 95% confidence level. Furthermore, it is argued in the analysis section that the 99% confidence level is the appropriate confidence level to reject the null hypothesis (Brace & Brace-Pellillo, 2009; Bonferroni, 1935, 1936).

The non-standardized estimate of the coefficient for product quality was .443 with a standard error of .082. The β-value was .332, the t-statistic was 5.388, and the p-value was .000. The estimated value of the coefficient for project team effectiveness was .473 with a standard error of .087, where the β-value was .344. The t-statistic was 5.441 and p-value was .000. Finally, the estimated value of the coefficient for project management effectiveness was equal to -.354 with a standard error was .076, and the β-value was -.280. The t-statistic was -4.678 and the p-value was .000. Similar to the results for the previous regression, these findings appeared to show that the non-standardized coefficients for product quality, project team effectiveness, and project management effectiveness are all statistically significant at the 99% confidence level.

Table 30 *Confidence Intervals for the Coefficients Using the Known Agile-Driven Projects and Known Plan-Driven Projects with a Dummy Variable*

Explanatory Variables	L.B. for 95% C.I.	U.B. for 95% C.I.	L.B. for 99% C.I.	U.B. for 99% C.I.
(Constant)	.449	2.422	.132	2.738
Dummy Variable	-.011	.356	-.071	.415
Product Quality	.281	.606	.229	.657
Project Team Effectiveness	.301	.644	.246	.700
Project Management Effectiveness	-.504	-.205	-.552	-.156

Note. The abbreviations are "L.B." for "Lower Bound", "U.B." for "Upper Bound", and "C.I." for "Confidence Interval".
Note. Customer Satisfaction was the dependent variable.
Note. The Dummy Variable equaled zero for known plan-driven projects and one for known agile-driven projects.

The results in Table 30 consist of the 95% and 99% confidence intervals. At the 95% confidence level, the confidence interval for the constant term was [.449, 2.422], whereas at the 99% confidence level the confidence interval was [.132, 2.738]. For the coefficient of the dummy variable, the confidence interval was [-.011, .356] at the 95% confidence level, whereas the confidence interval was [-.071, .415] at the 99% confidence level. Please note that at both the 95% and 99% confidence levels, zero is contained in both intervals.

For product quality, at the 95% confidence level, the confidence interval was [.281, .606], and at the 99% confidence level the confidence interval was [.229, .657]. When project team effectiveness was considered, at the 95% confidence level the confidence interval was [.301, .644], and at the 99% confidence level the confidence interval was [.246, .700]. Finally, as for project management effectiveness, at the 95% confidence level the confidence interval was [-.504, -.205], and at the 99% confidence level the confidence interval was [-.552, -.156].

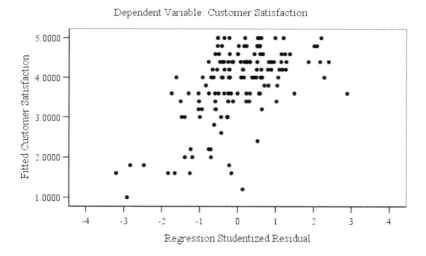

Figure 2. Residual Plot for the Regression with a Dummy Variable Using the Known Agile-Driven Projects and the Known Plan-Driven Projects

The scatter diagram for the residuals is contained in Figure 2. The horizontal axis represents the regression studentized residuals, and the vertical axis denotes the fitted customer satisfaction values. The values of the regression studentized residuals range from minus four to four, because the residuals approximate the standard normal distribution with a mean of zero and a standard deviation equal to one. The fitted customer satisfaction values range from one to five which corresponds to the 5-point Likert-type scales used to measure customer satisfaction. The circles in Figure 2 symbolize the values of the actual residuals.

Thus, from the residuals plotted in Figure 2, it seems that no heteroscedasticity appears to exist.

Table 31 *Correlation Matrix Using the Known Agile-Driven Projects and Known Plan-Driven Projects with a Dummy Variable*

Explanatory Variables	Dummy Variable	Product Quality	Project Team Effectiveness	Project Management Effectiveness
Dummy Variable		-.114	-.063	-.018
Product Quality			-.408**	.289**
Project Team Effectiveness				.370**
Project Management Effectiveness				

Note. Customer Satisfaction was the dependent variable.
Note. The Dummy Variable equaled zero for known plan-driven projects and one for known agile-driven projects.
Note. The double asterisk indicated that a correlation coefficient was statistically significant at the 99% confidence level.

In Table 31, the correlation for the first regression is presented in upper triangular form. There was minimal correlation between the dummy variable and product quality, project team effectiveness, and project management effectiveness. The correlations were -.114, -.063 and -.018 respectively. In contrast, the correlation between product quality and project team effectiveness was -.408, the correlation between product quality and project management effectiveness was .289, and the correlation between project team effectiveness and project management effectiveness was .370. Again, according to Brace and Brace-Pellillo (2009), when employing averaged variables in a regression equation, the correlations increase because the averaging process reduces variability. Therefore, although a correlation coefficient was statistically significant at the 99% confidence level, because the model was theoretically correct and because the *t*-statistics for the coefficients of the explanatory variables were statistically significant at the 99% confidence level, multicollinearity did not seem to be an issue.

Table 32 *Model Summary Using the Known Agile-Driven Projects and Known Plan-Driven Projects without a Dummy Variable*

Explanatory Variables	R	R Square	Adjusted R Square	Std. Error of the Estimate
(Constant)	.821	.674	.667	.5358603
Product Quality				
Project Team Effectiveness				
Project Management Effectiveness				

Note. Customer Satisfaction was the dependent variable.

In the second regression equation, Table 32 summarizes the results. The R-squared value was .674, showing that the constant term, product quality, project team effectiveness, and project management effectiveness explained 67.4% of the variance in customer satisfaction for known agile-driven and known plan-driven projects. The adjusted R-squared value was .667, implying that the model explained 66.7% of the variance in customer satisfaction, adjusted for the degrees of freedom. Because the actual R-squared value and the adjusted R-squared value was .007, this model has value when estimating customer satisfaction where the software development methodology is known.

Table 33 *Analysis of Variance Statistics Using the Known Agile-Driven Projects and Known Plan-Driven Projects without a Dummy Variable*

Source of Variation	Sum of Squares	df	Mean Square	F	Sig.
Regression	85.344	3	28.448	99.071	.000
Residual	41.439	144	.287		
Total	126.693	147			

Note. Customer Satisfaction was the dependent variable.
Note. The explanatory variables were: (Constant), Product Quality, Project Team Effectiveness, and Project Management Effectiveness.

Table 33 contains the ANOVA statistics, and the value of $F(3,144)$ was 99.071, where the p-value was .000. The two statistics suggested that the model is useful in estimating customer satisfaction for software development projects, and that there is a significant connection between customer satisfaction and product quality, project team effectiveness, and project management effectiveness.

Table 34 contains the results of the regression, including the non-standardized coefficients, the standardized coefficients, the values of the *t*-statistics, and the *p*-values. The estimated of the constant term, or autonomous customer satisfaction, was 1.441 with a standard error of .503, the value of the *t*-statistic was 2.863 and the *p*-value was .005. In other words, the constant term was significant at the 99% confidence level. The estimated of the coefficient for product quality was .460 with a standard error of .082. The *β*-value was .332, the *t*-statistic was 5.590, and the *p*-value was .000. The estimated value of the coefficient for project team effectiveness was .483 with a standard error of .087, where the *β*-value was .351. The *t*-statistic was 5.523 and *p*-value was .000. Finally, the estimated value of the coefficient for project management effectiveness was -.352 with a standard error was .076, and the *β*-value was -.278. The *t*-statistic was -4.607 and the *p*-value was .000. Like the results for the previous regression, these findings appeared to show that the coefficients for product quality, project team effectiveness, and project management effectiveness were all statistically significant at the 99% confidence level.

Table 34 *Regression Results Using the Known Agile-Driven Projects and Known Plan-Driven Projects without a Dummy Variable*

Explanatory Variables	Non-standardized Coefficients		Standardized Coefficients		
	B	Std. Error	Beta	t	Sig.
(Constant)	1.441	.503		2.863	.005
Product Quality	.460	.082	.345	5.590	.000
Project Team Effectiveness	.483	.087	.351	5.523	.000
Project Management Effectiveness	-.352	.076	-.278	-4.607	.000

Note. Customer Satisfaction was the dependent variable.

Table 35 consists of the 95% and 99% confidence intervals. At the 95% confidence level, the confidence interval for the constant term was [.446, 2.436], whereas at the 99% confidence level the confidence interval was [.128, 2.754]. For product quality, at the 95% confidence level, the confidence interval was [.298, .623], and at the 99% confidence level the confidence interval was [.246, .674]. When project team effectiveness was considered, at the 95% confidence level the confidence interval was [.310, .656], and at the 99% confidence level the confidence interval was [.256, .710]. Finally, as for project management

effectiveness, at the 95% confidence level the confidence interval was [-.503, -.201], and at
the 99% confidence level the confidence interval was [-.550, -.154].

Table 35 *Confidence Intervals for the Coefficients Using the Known Agile-Driven Projects
and Known Plan-Driven Projects without a Dummy Variable*

Explanatory Variables	L.B. for 95% C.I.	U.B. for 95% C.I.	L.B. for 99% C.I.	U.B. for 99% C.I.
(Constant)	.446	2.436	.128	2.754
Product Quality	.298	.623	.246	.674
Project Team Effectiveness	.310	.656	.256	.710
Project Management Effectiveness	-.503	-.201	-.550	-.154

Note. The abbreviations are "L.B." for "Lower Bound", "U.B." for "Upper Bound", and "C.I." for
"Confidence Interval".
Note. Customer Satisfaction was the dependent variable.

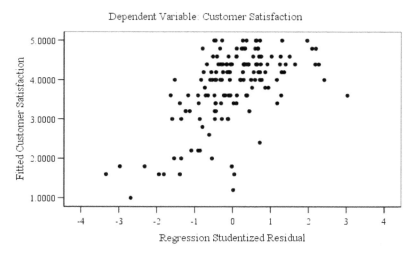

Figure 3. Residual Plot for the Regression without a Dummy Variable Using the Known
Agile-Driven Projects and the Known Plan-Driven Projects

For this regression equation, Figure 3 contains the residuals when plotted against the
fitted customer satisfaction values. Again, the horizontal axis represents the regression
studentized residuals, and the vertical axis denotes the fitted customer satisfaction values. The

values of the regression studentized residuals range from minus four to four, because the residuals ε approximate the standard normal distribution with mean of zero and a standard deviation equal to one. The fitted customer satisfaction values range from one to five which corresponds to the 5-point Likert-type scales used to measure customer satisfaction. The circles in Figure 3 stand for the values of the actual residuals. Therefore, from the residuals plotted in Figure 3, it appears that no heteroscedasticity exists.

Table 36 *Correlation Matrix Using the Known Agile-Driven Projects and Known Plan-Driven Projects without a Dummy Variable*

Explanatory Variables	Product Quality	Project Team Effectiveness	Project Management Effectiveness
Product Quality		-.419**	.289**
Project Team Effectiveness			.370**
Project Management Effectiveness			

Note. Customer Satisfaction was the dependent variable.
Note. The double asterisk indicated that a correlation coefficient was statistically significant at the 99% confidence level.
Note. The Dummy Variable equaled zero for known plan-driven plus probable plan-driven projects and one for known agile-driven plus probable agile-driven projects.

In Table 36, the correlation matrix for the second regression equation is presented in upper triangular form. The correlation between product quality and project team effectiveness was -.419, the correlation between product quality and project management effectiveness was .289, and the correlation between project team effectiveness and project management effectiveness was .370. Again, according to Brace and Brace-Pellillo (2009), when employing averaged variables in a regression equation, the correlations increased because the averaging process reduces variability. Therefore, although a correlation coefficient was statistically significant at the 99% confidence level, because the model was theoretically correct and because the *t*-statistics for the coefficients of the explanatory variables were statistically significant at the 99% confidence level, multicollinearity did not appear to be an issue.

Table 37 *Means, Medians, and Standard Deviations for the Dependent and Explanatory*
Variables when the Software Development Methodology Is Known or Inferred

Known plus Probable Agile-Driven and Plan-Driven Projects	Count	Means	Medians	Standard Deviations
Known Agile-Driven plus Probable Agile-Driven Projects				
Customer Satisfaction	119	3.872	4.024	.826
Product Quality	119	3.325	3.399	.677
Project Team Effectiveness	119	3.924	4.000	.686
Project Management Effectiveness	119	2.895	2.768	.755
Known Plan-Driven plus Probable Plan-Driven Projects				
Customer Satisfaction	66	3.467	3.653	1.022
Product Quality	66	3.071	3.125	.704
Project Team Effectiveness	66	3.747	3.798	.701
Project Management Effectiveness	66	3.019	2.923	.673

Known plus Probable Software Development Methodologies. Before showing the
two regressions when the software development methodology was known or inferred, the
means, medians, and the standard deviations for customer satisfaction, product quality,
project team effectiveness, and project management effectiveness variables are displayed in
Table 37. In the table, the data are separated by whether the software development
methodology was known or inferred to be agile-driven or plan-driven. The means and
medians for the agile-driven projects are again larger than the means and medians for the
plan-driven projects, whereas the standard deviations for the agile-driven projects are less
than the standard deviations for the plan-driven projects.

Table 38 *Model Summary Using Known Agile-Driven plus Probable Agile-Driven Projects and Known Plan-Driven plus Probable Plan-Driven Projects with a Dummy Variable*

Explanatory Variables	R	R Square	Adjusted R Square	Std. Error of the Estimate
(Constant)	.820	.672	.665	.5322667
Dummy Variable				
Product Quality				
Project Team Effectiveness				
Project Management Effectiveness				

Note. Customer Satisfaction was the dependent variable.

The statistics in Table 38 summarize the results of the regression. The R-squared value was .672, indicating that the constant term, the dummy variable, product quality, project team effectiveness, and project management effectiveness accounted for 67.2% of the variance in customer satisfaction. The adjusted R-squared value is the multiple coefficient of determination corrected for the degrees of freedom. In general, greater the number of explanatory variables, the greater is the downward adjustment. In this case, the adjusted R-squared value of .665 indicated that the model explained 66.5% of the variance in customer satisfaction, adjusted for the degrees of freedom. Because the difference between the actual R-squared value and the adjusted R-squared value was .007, it is concluded that the model is rather valuable in estimating customer satisfaction.

Table 39 *Analysis of Variance Statistics Using Known Agile-Driven plus Probable Agile-Driven Projects and Known Plan-Driven plus Probable Plan-Driven Projects with a Dummy Variable*

Source of Variation	Sum of Squares	df	Mean Square	F	Sig.
Regression	104.394	4	26.098	92.121	.000
Residual	50.995	180	.283		
Total	155.389	184			

Note. Customer Satisfaction was the dependent variable.
Note. The explanatory variables were: (Constant), Dummy Variable, Product Quality, Project Team Effectiveness, and Project Management Effectiveness.
Note. The Dummy Variable equaled zero for known plan-driven plus probable plan-driven projects and one for known agile-driven plus probable agile-driven projects.

Table 39 contains the analysis of variance (ANOVA) statistics, and the value of $F_{(4,180)}$ was 92.121 where the p-value was less than .0005. These two statistics indicated that the model is quite useful in estimating customer satisfaction for software development projects, and that there is a high degree of association between customer satisfaction and product quality, project team effectiveness, and project management effectiveness.

Table 40 *Regression Results Using Known Agile-Driven plus Probable Agile-Driven Projects and Known Plan-Driven plus Probable Plan-Driven Projects with a Dummy Variable*

Explanatory Variables	Non-standardized Coefficients		Standardized Coefficients		
	B	Std. Error	Beta	t	Sig.
(Constant)	1.233	.435		2.832	.005
Dummy Variable	.165	.083	.086	1.991	.048
Product Quality	.474	.073	.358	6.472	.000
Project Team Effectiveness	.461	.074	.348	6.240	.000
Project Management Effectiveness	-.314	.067	-.248	-4.653	.000

Note. Customer Satisfaction was the dependent variable.
Note. The Dummy Variable equaled zero for known plan-driven plus probable plan-driven projects and one for known agile-driven plus probable agile-driven projects.

Table 40 lists the results of the non-standardized coefficients, the standardized coefficients, the values of the t-statistics, and the p-values. The estimated value of the constant term, or the level of autonomous customer satisfaction, was 1.233 with a standard error of .435, the value of the t-statistic was 2.832, and the p-value was .005. In other words, the constant term was significant at the 99% confidence level. For the dummy variable, the estimated value of the coefficient was .165 with a standard error of .083, the β-value equaled .086, the t-statistic was 1.991, and the p-value was .048. This means that the coefficient of the dummy variable was barely statistically significant at the 95% confidence level, but statistically insignificant at the 99% confidence level. This result was examined in greater detail when the findings are analyzed. It is argued in the analysis section of this chapter that the 99% confidence level was more appropriate because all of the variables in the regression equation were averages, and averaged variables reduced the variation when used in regressions (Brace & Brace-Pellillo, 2009).

The estimated value of the coefficient for product quality was .474 with a standard error of .073. The β-value was .358 with a t-statistic of 6.472 and a p-value of .000. The estimated value of the coefficient for project team effectiveness was .461 with a standard error of .074, where the β-value was .348. The t-statistic was 6.240 and the p-value was .000. Finally, the estimated value of the coefficient for project management effectiveness was -.314 with a standard error of .067, and β-value was -.248. The t-statistic was -4.653 and the p-value was .000. These results indicate that the coefficients for product quality, project team effectiveness, and project management effectiveness were all statistically significant at the 99% confidence level.

Table 41 *Confidence Intervals for the Coefficients Using Known Agile-Driven plus Probable Agile-Driven Projects and Known Plan-Driven plus Probable Plan-Driven Projects with a Dummy Variable*

Explanatory Variables	L.B. for 95% C.I.	U.B. for 95% C.I.	L.B. for 99% C.I.	U.B. for 99% C.I.
(Constant)	.374	2.091	.101	2.365
Dummy Variable	.001	.329	-.051	.381
Product Quality	.329	.618	.284	.664
Project Team Effectiveness	.315	.607	.268	.654
Project Management Effectiveness	-.447	-.181	-.488	-.140

Note. The abbreviations are "L.B." for "Lower Bound", "U.B." for "Upper Bound", and "C.I." for "Confidence Interval".
Note. Customer Satisfaction was the dependent variable.
Note. The Dummy Variable equaled zero for known plan-driven plus probable plan-driven projects and one for known agile-driven plus probable agile-driven projects.

Table 41 includes the 95% and 99% confidence intervals. The confidence interval for the constant term was [.374, 2.091] at the 95% confidence level, whereas at the 99% confidence level the confidence interval was [.101, 2.365]. For the dummy variable, at the 95% confidence level the confidence interval was [.001, .329], and at the 99% confidence level, the confidence interval was [-.051, .381]. Please note that at the 95% confidence level, the lower bound was almost zero, and that at the 99% confidence level, zero was included in the interval. This result was consistent with the conclusion that the dummy variable was barely statistically significant at the 95% confidence level, but statistically insignificant at the 99% confidence level.

Dependent Variable: Customer Satisfaction

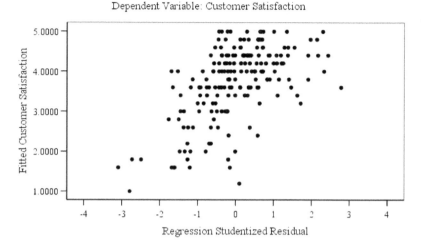

Figure 4. Residual Plot for the Regression with a Dummy Variable Using the Known Agile-Driven plus Probable Agile-Driven Projects and the Known Plan-Driven plus Probable Plan-Driven Projects

For product quality, at the 95% confidence level the confidence interval was [.329, .618], and at the 99% confidence level the confidence interval was [.284, .664]. When project team effectiveness is considered, at the 95% confidence level the confidence interval was [.315, .607], and at the 99% confidence level the confidence interval was [.268, .654]. Finally, as for project management effectiveness, at the 95% confidence level the confidence interval was [-.447, -.181], and at the 99% confidence level the confidence interval was [-.488, -.140].

Figure 4 displays the residuals when the data from known agile-driven plus probable agile-driven projects and known plan-driven plus probable plan-driven projects are employed. Similar to what has appeared in Figures 2 and 3, there is no apparent to adjust the non-standardized estimates of the coefficients for the presence of heteroscedasticity.

In Table 42, the correlation matrix is presented in upper triangular form. There was minimal correlation between the dummy variable and product quality, project team effectiveness, and project management effectiveness. The correlations were -.130, -.031, and -.021 respectively. In contrast, the correlation between product quality and project team effectiveness was -.404, the correlation between product quality and project management effectiveness was .302, and the correlation between project team effectiveness and project management effectiveness was .348. According to Brace and Brace-Pellillo (2009), in regression analysis the correlations between averaged variables tend to increase because the averaging process reduces variability. Thus, even though a correlation coefficient was statistically significant at the 99% confidence level, because the model was theoretically correct and because the t-statistics for the dummy variable and the coefficients of the explanatory variables are statistically significant at the 95% and 99% confidence levels, multicollinearity does not seem to be an issue.

Table 42 *Correlation Matrix Using Known Agile-Driven plus Probable Agile-Driven Projects and Known Plan-Driven plus Probable Plan-Driven Projects with a Dummy Variable*

Explanatory Variables	Dummy Variable	Product Quality	Project Team Effectiveness	Project Management Effectiveness
Dummy Variable		-.130	-.031	-.021
Product Quality			-404**	.302**
Project Team Effectiveness				.348**
Project Management Effectiveness				

Note. Customer Satisfaction was the dependent variable.
Note. The Dummy Variable equaled zero for known plan-driven plus probable plan-driven projects and one for known agile-driven plus probable agile-driven projects.
Note. The double asterisk indicated that a correlation coefficient was statistically significant at the 99% confidence level.

The statistics in Table 43 summarize the results of the regression without a dummy variable. The R-squared value was .665, indicating that the constant term, the dummy variable, product quality, project team effectiveness, and project management effectiveness accounted for 66.5% of the variance in customer satisfaction. The adjusted R-squared value is the multiple coefficient of determination corrected for the degrees of freedom. In general, greater the number of explanatory variables, the greater was the downward adjustment. In this case, the adjusted R-squared value of .659 indicated that the model explained 65.9% of the variance in customer satisfaction, adjusted for the degrees of freedom. Because the difference between the actual R-squared value and the adjusted R-squared value was .006, it is concluded that the model is quite helpful in estimating customer satisfaction.

Table 43 *Model Summary Using Known Agile-Driven plus Probable Agile-Driven Projects and Known Plan-Driven plus Probable Plan-Driven Projects without a Dummy Variable*

Explanatory Variables	R	R Square	Adjusted R Square	Std. Error of the Estimate
(Constant)	.815	.665	.659	.5366047
Dummy Variable				
Product Quality				
Project Team Effectiveness				
Project Management Effectiveness				

Note. Customer Satisfaction was the dependent variable.
Note. The Dummy Variable equaled zero for known plan-driven plus probable plan-driven projects and one for known agile-driven plus probable agile-driven projects.

Table 44 contains the analysis of variance (ANOVA) statistics, and the value of $F(3,181)$ was 119.550 where the p-value was less than .0005. These two statistics indicated that the model is rather useful in estimating customer satisfaction for software development projects, and that there is a high degree of association between customer satisfaction and product quality, project team effectiveness, and project management effectiveness.

Table 44 *Analysis of Variance Statistics Using Known Agile-Driven plus Probable Agile-Driven Projects and Known Plan-Driven plus Probable Plan-Driven Projects without a Dummy Variable*

Source of Variation	Sum of Squares	df	Mean Square	F	Sig.
Regression	103.271	3	34.424	119.550	.000
Residual	52.118	181	.288		
Total	155.389	184			

Note. Customer Satisfaction was the dependent variable.
Note. The explanatory variables were: (Constant), Product Quality, Project Team Effectiveness, and Project Management Effectiveness.

Table 45 lists the results of the non-standardized coefficients, the standardized coefficients, the values of the t-statistics, and the p-values. The estimated value of the constant term, or the level of autonomous customer satisfaction, was 1.251 with a standard error of .439, the value of the t-statistic was 2.853, and the p-value was .005. In other words, the constant term was significant at the 99% confidence level. The estimated value of the coefficient for product quality was .492 with a standard error of .073. The β-value was .373

with a *t*-statistic of 6.734 and a *p*-value of .000. The estimated value of the coefficient for project team effectiveness was .465 with a standard error of .074, where the β-value was .352. The *t*-statistic was 6.254 and the *p*-value was .000. Finally, the estimated value of the coefficient for project management effectiveness was -.311 with a standard error of .068, and β-value was -.246. The *t*-statistic was -4.574 and the *p*-value was .000. These results indicated that the coefficients for product quality, project team effectiveness, and project management effectiveness were all statistically significant at the 99% confidence level.

Table 45 *Regression Results Using Known Agile-Driven plus Probable Agile-Driven Projects and Known Plan-Driven plus Probable Plan-Driven Projects without a Dummy Variable*

Explanatory Variables	Non-standardized Coefficients		Standardized Coefficients		
	B	Std. Error	Beta	t	Sig.
(Constant)	1.251	.439		2.853	.005
Product Quality	.492	.073	.373	6.734	.000
Project Team Effectiveness	.465	.074	.352	6.254	.000
Project Management Effectiveness	-.311	.068	-.246	-4.574	.000

Note. Customer Satisfaction was the dependent variable.

Table 46 includes the 95% confidence intervals and the 99% confidence intervals. The confidence interval for the constant term was [.386, 2.117] at the 95% confidence level, whereas at the 99% confidence level the confidence interval was [.108, 2.394]. For product quality, at the 95% confidence level the confidence interval was [.348, .637], and at the 99% confidence level the confidence interval was [.302, .684]. When project team effectiveness was considered, at the 95% confidence level the confidence interval was [.319, .612], and at the 99% confidence level the confidence interval was [.272, .658]. Finally, as for project management effectiveness, at the 95% confidence level the confidence interval was [-.445, -.177], and at the 99% confidence level the confidence interval was [-.488, -.1434].

Table 46 *Confidence Intervals for the Coefficients Using Known Agile-Driven plus Probable Agile-Driven Projects and Known Plan-Driven plus Probable Plan-Driven Projects without a Dummy Variable*

Explanatory Variables	L.B. for 95% C.I.	U.B. for 95% C.I.	L.B. for 99% C.I.	U.B. for 99% C.I.
(Constant)	.386	2.117	.108	2.394
Product Quality	.348	.637	.302	.684
Project Team Effectiveness	.319	.612	.272	.658
Project Management Effectiveness	-.445	-.177	-.488	-.134

Note. The abbreviations are "L.B." for "Lower Bound", "U.B." for "Upper Bound", and "C.I." for "Confidence Interval".
Note. Customer Satisfaction was the dependent variable.

Figure 5 shows the residuals plotted against the fitted values for customer satisfaction when the dummy variable is removed from the model. As previously discussed, there appears to be no heteroscedasticity in this version of the regression equation.

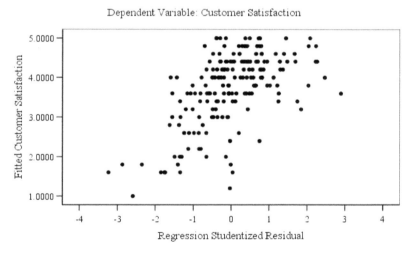

Figure 5. Residual Plot for the Regression without a Dummy Variable Using the Known Agile-Driven plus Probable Agile-Driven Projects and the Known Plan-Driven plus Probable Plan-Driven Projects

In Table 47, the correlation matrix is presented in upper triangular form. The correlation between product quality and project team effectiveness was -.412, the correlation between product quality and project management effectiveness was .302, and the correlation between project team effectiveness and project management effectiveness was .348. According to Brace and Brace-Pellillo (2009), in regression analysis the correlations between averaged variables tended to increase because the averaging process reduces variability. Thus, even though a correlation coefficient was statistically significant at the 99% confidence level, because the model was theoretically correct and because the t-statistics for the explanatory variables were statistically significant at the 99% confidence levels, multicollinearity did not appear to be an issue.

Table 47 *Correlation Matrix Using Known Agile-Driven plus Probable Agile-Driven Projects and Known Plan-Driven plus Probable Plan-Driven Projects without a Dummy Variable*

Explanatory Variables	Product Quality	Project Team Effectiveness	Project Management Effectiveness
Product Quality		-.412**	.302**
Project Team Effectiveness			.348**
Project Management Effectiveness			

Note. Customer Satisfaction was the dependent variable.
Note. The double asterisk indicated that a correlation coefficient was statistically significant at the 99% confidence level.

Some Comments from the Participants

In the last section of the questionnaire, a participant had the opportunity to provide any additional comments about the project that he or she reported. Table 48 contained the counts and percentages of the individuals who contributed his or her comments. From Tab le 48, 51 respondents provided supplemental comments, whereas 134 respondents chose not to enter any comments. Of the 119 agile-driven plus probable projects, 33 participants elected to give further insights into these projects, and 86 participants decided to leave this section of the survey blank. For the known plan-driven plus probable plan-driven projects, 18 participants made additional comments available, and 48 participants preferred not to indulge. In terms of percentages, only 27.6% of all of the participants chose to enter additional comments, and 72.4% decided to refrain. These percentages were nearly identical for known agile-driven plus probable agile-driven projects and known plan-driven plus probable plan-driven projects.

Table 48 *Counts and Percentages of Participants Providing Additional Comments*

Participants Providing Additional Comments	All Projects	Known Agile-Driven plus Probable Agile-Driven Projects	Known Plan-Driven plus Probable Plan-Driven Projects
	Count (Percent)	Count (Percent)	Count (Percent)
Provided Additional Comments	51 (27.6%)	33 (27.7%)	18 (27.3%)
Did Not Provide Additional Comments	134 (72.4%)	86 (72.3%)	48 (72.7%)
Total	185 (100.0%)	119 (100.0%)	66 (100.0%)

For the remainder of this sub-section, the comments stemming from the participants that engaged in projects that employed agile-driven and plan-driven software development methodologies are highlighted. The intent was to further understand the issues that were perceived by the participants of this study.

Known Agile-Driven plus Probable Agile-Driven Projects. First, several participants wished the researcher good luck with this study. Some participants believed that Scrum was an effective agile-driven methodology, while other participants questioned the effectiveness of agile-driven methods because what occurred looked more like hacking than strict agile practices. One respondent remarked that the changing scope of the project prevented the project from achieving the planned budget with false starts being a critical issue. Another respondent used a customized blend of extreme programming and Scrum to achieve success, whereas another respondent stated that his or her project team used the term "agile methods" as a buzzword without understanding its meaning. Still another participant believed that the questions in the survey did not correspond with how projects operated in the real world. One participant argued that he or she provided data on a critical software development project, and that Scrum was outstandingly successful. Finally, two participants felt that it was the enthusiasm of the project team that made the difference, and not the use of agile-driven methods. One of these two respondents was employed in a CMM organization that successfully used agile-driven methods to achieve success.

Known Plan-Driven plus Probable Plan-Driven Projects. Like the respondents that were engaged in known agile-driven plus probable agile-driven projects, several individuals hoped that the research went well. One participant noted that agile software development methods do not cover database design. Another respondent successfully employed plan-driven methods on a software development project that was two and a half years late and was within 10% of its new budget and schedule. A third participant observed that project management methodologies should not be confused with administrative methodologies. Still another participant noticed that the questionnaire did not address cultural issues, particularly when Chinese-Asian management practices were contrasted with European management practices. One participant wanted question 48 regarding the major roles that a person played in a project to allow for multiple entries. Another respondent believed that the project was successful due to good leadership on the part of the project manager, and not the software development used. Still another participant stated that the requirements were well specified, that being the major reason why the project was successful. Finally, two respondents wanted to know why the specific occupation of software development engineer was not listed.

Analysis of the Findings

Software Development Methodologies

In the section, the frequencies of the various software development methodologies that make up the data are analyzed. From Table 3, there were 95 agile-driven projects, 53 plan-driven projects, and 37 projects where the software development methodology employed was not known. The fact that 51.4% of the participants were engaged in agile-driven projects may be due to the ease in which the agile community took the internet survey contained in Appendix C. In contrast, 28.6% of the participants reported on plan-driven projects, reflecting the fact that it was much more difficult to contact these individuals. Finally, 20.0% of the respondents did not know the specific software development methodology that was used in the project that was the subject of his or her data. This means that for a substantial number of participants, the particular software development methodology was not sufficiently important to remember when the questionnaire was being taken.

A breakdown of the various agile-driven methodologies is provided in Table 4, where 58 or 53.2% of the projects employed the Extreme Programming and 23 or 21.1% of the projects used Scrum. Furthermore, there were five Feature Driven Development projects, two Crystal Methods projects, and 21 projects that either utilized a homegrown method or combined different agile-driven methods together. In this study, 12 or 12.4% of the participants indicated that he or she used Extreme Programming, 58 or 61.1% of the respondents employed Scrum, two projects utilized Feature Driven Development, two projects used Lean Development, and none of the projects employed Crystal Methods or Dynamic Systems Development. There were nine projects that either utilized a homegrown method or comingled various agile-driven methodologies. Finally, eight participants indicated that an agile-driven methodology was employed in the project, but he or she was not sure what specific methodology was used.

Cao (2006) analyzed the critical success factors in the 109 agile-driven projects that formed the basis of his study. Because Cao's (2006) data are two years older than the data in this study, the reason for the percentage differences between Extreme Programming and Scrum could be due to an increasing acceptance of Scrum in the agile-driven community, and a relative decline in the popularity of Extreme Programming. As for the other agile-driven methods, it could be that these methods will eventually disappear as Scrum, the apparent dominant software development methodology, crowds out the other agile-driven methods (Utterback, 1996). What is needed is additional research to verify this proposition. Although an attempt was made to find frequency data similar to what was found in Cao's (2006) study, no such data were discovered.

When considering the 53 plan-driven projects listed in Table 5, 29 or 54.3% of the projects consisted of the Capability Maturity Model, the Capability Maturity Model Integration, the Personal Software Process, or the Team Software Process. These four plan-driven software development methodologies originated at Carnegie-Mellon University (Paulk et al, 1994; Humphrey, 1996, 1999). The reason that these plan-driven methodologies were so highly represented was because 137 SPIN organizations were contacted, 50 resided in the United Sates and 87 were located internationally. There were five projects that used the Software Factory methodology, and 11 projects employing miscellaneous methodologies, including Military Standards, the ISO Standard, the EIA Standard, and the IEEE Standard. Furthermore, four of the projects either utilized a homegrown method, or combined various plan-driven methodologies together. Finally, five participants stated that he or she knew that a plan-driven software development methodology was used, but did know specifically which method was employed. In other words, given the age of the Carnegie-Mellon brand of software development, it appears to be the dominant plan-driven software development methodology, having crowding out any and all would be competitors (Utterback, 1996).

The 37 participants that did not know what software development methodology was employed remain to be analyzed. The results from Table 6 indicated that 24 or 64.9% of the participants were probably involved in agile-driven projects, whereas 13 or 35.1% of the respondents were likely involved in plan-driven projects. The ratio of probable agile-driven projects to probable plan-driven projects is 1.85, and the ratio of known agile-driven projects to known plan-driven projects is 1.79 with a variance of .06. From a qualitative perspective, this result seemed to indicate that combining known agile-driven projects with probable agile-driven projects and known plan-driven projects with probable plan-driven projects was reasonable to do.

Characteristics of the Projects

Before evaluating the results of the regressions, the characteristics of the projects that made up the study followed by the characteristics of the participants who responded to the survey are examined in order to gain a better understanding of the data. Rather than dwell on the frequency tables that that were previously presented, the means, medians, and standard deviations of these characteristics were the focus of the succeeding analysis.

Size of the Projects. From Table 15, the mean number of person hours expended for known agile-driven plus probable agile-driven projects was 2,303 person hours, where the median was 1,737 person hours and where the standard deviation was 1,032 person hours. In contrast, Table 16 showed that the average number of person hours expended for plan-driven plus probable plan driven projects was 5,273 person hours, where the median was 5,556 person hours and where the standard deviation was 1,127 person hours. The coefficient of dispersion for agile-driven plus agile-driven projects was .448, whereas the coefficient of dispersion for known plan-driven plus probable plan-driven projects was .214. This means that in terms of the number of person hours expended, there was a wider range of known agile-driven plus probable agile-driven projects than known plan-driven plus probable plan-driven projects. A difference of means test was conducted on the two data sets using the non-pooled t-test for two population means with unequal variances (Kutner et al., 2004). The value of the t-statistic was 17.688 with 79 degrees of freedom using the Welch-Satterthwaitte equation, and was statistically significant at the 99% confidence level (Satterthwaitte, 1946; Welch, 1947). In other words, in terms of the number of person hours expended, known agile-driven plus probable agile-driven projects were significantly smaller than plan-driven plus probable plan driven projects.

From Table 15, the average number of project team members for known agile-driven plus probable agile-driven projects was 7.9 individuals with a median of 5.1 individuals and a standard deviation of 2.6 individuals. From Table 16, the average number of project team members for known plan-driven plus probable plan-driven projects was 16.7 individuals with a median of 9.1 individuals and a standard deviation of 10.9 individuals. The coefficient of dispersion for agile-driven plus agile-driven projects was .329, whereas the coefficient of dispersion for known plan-driven plus probable plan-driven projects was .653. This means that in terms of the number of project team members, there were a wider range of known plan-driven plus probable plan-driven projects than known agile-driven plus probable agile-driven projects. In other words, there were a rather large number of relatively small known plan-driven plus probable plan-driven projects when the number of project team members is the characteristic that determines project size in the minds of the participants. Again, a difference of means test was carried out using the non-pooled t-test for two population means with unequal variances (Kutner et al., 2004). The value of the t-statistic was 6.458 with 6 degrees of freedom using the Welch-Satterthwaitte equation, and was statistically significant at the 99% confidence level (Satterthwaitte, 1946; Welch, 1947). In other words, in terms of the number of individuals in a project team, known agile-driven plus probable agile-driven projects were significantly smaller than known plan-driven plus probable plan-driven projects.

Although Highsmith (2004) and Schwaber (2004) stated that agile-driven projects are typically small projects, the meaning of the word "small" is unclear. To provide greater clarity, and to see if the words of these two authors could be substantiated, Cao (2006) provided a frequency table of the number individuals engaged in the 109 projects in his study. When the mean, median, and standard deviation were calculated and then converted, it turned out that the mean number of project members was 8.4 individuals, where the median was 5.1 individuals and the standard deviation was 3.6 individuals. A difference of means test was performed using the non-pooled t-test for two population means with unequal variances, where Cao's (2006) results were compared with the results from this study (Kutner et al., 2004). The value of the t-statistic was 1.193 with 43 degrees of freedom using the Welch-Satterthwaitte equation, and was statistically insignificant at the 95% confidence level (Satterthwaitte, 1946; Welch, 1947). In other words, in terms of the number of individuals in an agile-driven project team, there were no statistically significant differences between the results in Cao's (2006) study and this study. This means that there was evidence to suggest that the mean number of individuals in known agile-driven plus probable agile-driven project teams found by this study was reasonable. Unfortunately, no frequency data on the number of project team members were found for plan-driven software development projects

When budgeted dollars amounts for the 185 projects contained in this study are analyzed, an interesting picture is revealed. From Table 15, for known agile-driven plus probable agile-driven projects the mean budgeted dollar amount was $155,455 with a median value of $128,125 and a standard deviation of $50,395. From Table 16, the average budgeted dollar amount for known plan-driven plus probable plan-driven projects was $238,630 with a median value of $250,000 and a standard deviation of $57,170. The coefficient of dispersion for known agile-driven plus probable agile-driven projects was .324, and the coefficient of dispersion for known plan-driven plus probable plan-driven projects was .240. This means that in terms of the budgeted dollar amounts, there was a wider range of known agile-driven plus probable agile-driven projects than known plan-driven plus probable plan-driven projects. For a third time, a difference of means test was calculated out using the non-pooled t-test for two population means with unequal variances (Kutner et al., 2004). The value of the t-statistic was 9.881 with 145 degrees of freedom using the Welch-Satterthwaitte equation, and was statistically significant at the 99% confidence level (Satterthwaitte, 1946; Welch, 1947). In other words, in terms of budgeted dollar amounts, there was a statistically significant difference between known agile-driven plus probable agile-driven projects and known plan-driven plus probable plan-driven projects. Thus, the evidence suggested that the known plan-driven plus probable plan-driven projects were definitely more expensive than the known agile-driven plus probable agile-driven projects.

According to Schwalbe (2006), many information technology projects "do not have good planning information, so tracking performance against a plan produce misleading information" (p. 275). Furthermore, Fleming and Koppleman (2000) pointed out that a project's true cost performance cannot be determined. Kerzner (2006) aptly observed that most people have a poor understanding of cost control, because many organizations do not possess a well-organized and well-managed cost control system. Meredith and Mantel (2003) noticed that the "longer the project life cycle, the less the PM can trust that traditional methods and costs will be relevant" (p. 337). Thus, for this study, it was decided not collect actual cost data for the projects analyzed in the study, but rather estimate the cost of the projects based upon risk factors (Cooper et al., 2005). Essentially, any actual cost data that the study could have collected would have probably been inaccurate at best or just plain wrong at worst.

Question 41 attempted to qualify the actual costs of a project by asking whether a software development projects was significantly under budget, under budget, approximately on budget, over budget or significantly over budget. The idea is that a participant would have a clear qualitative understanding of the cost of a project rather than a quantitative notion in terms of dollars and cents. The frequency results appear in Table 47.

From Table 49, none of the 185 projects in the study completed significantly under budget. Of the 18 projects that were completed under budget, 13 projects were known agile-driven or probable agile-driven, and five projects were known plan-driven or probable plan-driven. One hundred eight of the 185 projects were finished approximately on budget, where 67 projects were known agile-driven or probable agile-driven, and 41 projects were known plan-driven or probable plan-driven. Of the 49 projects that were over budget, 34 projects were known agile-driven or probable agile-driven, and 15 projects were known plan-driven or probable plan-driven. Finally, 10 projects were significantly over budget, five of which were known agile-driven or probable agile-driven, and five of which were known plan-driven or probable plan-driven.

Table 49 *Projects Completed Under, On, or Over Budget*

Project Completed Under, On, or Over Budget	All Projects	Known Agile-Driven plus Probable Agile-Driven Projects	Known Plan-Driven plus Probable Plan-Driven Projects
	Count (Percent)	Count (Percent)	Count (Percent)
Significantly under Budget	0 (0.0%)	0 (0.0%)	0 (0.0%)
Under Budget	18 (9.7%)	13 (10.9%)	5 (7.6%)
Approximately on Budget	108 (58.4%)	67 (56.3%)	41 (62.1%)
Over Budget	49 (26.5%)	34 (28.6%)	15 (22.7%)
Significantly over Budget	10 (5.4%)	5 (4.2%)	5 (7.6%)
Total	185 (100.0%)	119 (100.0%)	66 (100.0%)

Cooper et al. (2005) provided 5-point Likert-type risk factors on cost increases. The first cost factor was .1, or insignificant, when the budget estimates were not exceeded and some transfer of money occurred. The second cost factor was .3, or low, when the project cost estimates exceeded the budget by 1-5%. The third cost factor was .5, or moderate, when the project cost estimates increased by 5-10%. The fourth cost factor was .7, or very high, when the estimate of the project cost increased by 10-20%. The fifth and last cost factor was .9, or catastrophic, when the estimated cost of a project was greater than 20%.

Table 50 *Estimated Means, Medians, and Standard Deviations of the Actual Project Costs*

Estimated Means, Medians, and Standard Deviations	All Projects	Known Agile-Driven plus Probable Agile-Driven Projects	Known Plan-Driven plus Probable Plan-Driven Projects
Estimated Actual Cost Mean Values	$199,501	$167,277	$257,792
Estimated Actual Cost Median Values	$179,976	$137,869	$270,075
Estimated Actual Cost Standard Deviation Values	$57,578	$54,228	$61,761

Note. The medians were calculated from grouped data.

The next step is to associate the 5-point Likert-type scale contained in question 41 with the 5-point Likert-type scale given by Cooper et al. (2005). Thus, it is posited that a software development project is approximately on budget if the actual cost is ±5% of the budgeted cost. The project is assumed to be under budget if the actual cost is between -15% and -6% of the budgeted cost, and over budget if the actual cost of the project is between 6% and 15% of the budgeted cost. Finally, a project is presumed to be significantly under budget if the actual cost is 16% or less than the budgeted cost, and significantly over budget if the actual cost is 16% or more than the budgeted cost. This proposed association appeared to be consistent with the 5-point Likert-type scale offered in Cooper et al. (2005).

When the means, medians, and standard deviations for question 41 on a 5-point Likert-type scale are combined with the estimated cost factors assumed above (i.e., 15% over budget), the results are quite interesting, and appear in Table 50. In order to understand how the figures in Table 50 were calculated, an example is helpful. In terms of the 5-point Likert-type scale for question 41, the mean value for all 185 projects was 3.2757. This number said that the average project in the study was slightly over budget. The decimal portion of the mean value above is .2757, the distance between 6% and 15% is 10%, and thus the resulting growth rate is .05 + (.1*.2757) = .07757. From Table 16, the average value for the budgeted dollar amount for all 185 projects is $185,140. The factor 1.07757 is then multiplied by $185,140 with the result being $199,501 rounded to near dollar. It is noted that among other things, the figures in Table 48 are dependent upon the responses of the participants to question six. If the respondents were unaware or understated the actual budgeted dollar amounts, then the estimated figures in Table 50 are probably smaller than the actual monies spent. Thus, it is assumed in the succeeding paragraphs that the responses to question six are accurate.

Given the analysis above of the size of the projects, one question that begs to be answered is whether agile-driven projects are more or less expensive than plan-driven projects. From the data, the question could have been answered from the vantage point of person hours or dollar amounts. Table 51 contains the mean person hours expended, the mean budgeted dollar amounts, and the estimated mean actual dollar amounts, all divided by the mean number project team members for all projects, known agile-driven plus probable agile-driven projects, and known plan-driven plus probable plan-driven projects. Thus, from Table 51, it was evident that the mean number of person hours per person for known agile-driven plus probable agile-driven projects was 291.5 person hours, whereas the mean number of person hours per person for known plan-driven plus probable plan-driven projects was 315.7 person hours. In other words, in terms of person hours expended, on the average an individual engaged in known agile-driven plus probable agile-driven projects spent 24.4 less person hours than a comparable person involved in known plan-driven plus probable plan-driven projects. From this information, it could be construed that individuals that labor in agile-driven software development projects were slightly more productive than their plan-driven counterparts.

When the mean budgeted dollar amounts per person for known agile-driven plus probable agile-driven projects were compared to the mean budgeted dollar amounts per person for known plan-driven plus probable plan-driven projects, the difference was $5,389. When the estimated mean actual dollars amounts were employed, the difference was $5,737. In other words, agile-driven software development projects had larger budgeted cost dollar amounts per project team member or larger estimated actual cost dollar amounts than known plan-driven plus probable plan-driven projects.

Table 51 *Mean Person Hour Expended per Person, Mean Budgeted Dollar Amount per Person, and Estimated Actual Dollar Amount per Person*

Mean Project Ratios	All Projects	Known Agile-Driven plus Probable Agile-Driven Projects	Known Plan-Driven plus Probable Plan-Driven Projects
Mean Person Hours Expended per Person	285.0 p.h.	291.5 p.h.	315.7 p.h.
Mean Budgeted Dollar Amounts per Person	$16,831	$19,678	$14,289
Estimated Mean Actual Dollar Amounts per Person	$18,136	$21,174	$15,437

Note. The abbreviation "p.h." stands for "person hours".
Note. The figures in the table were calculated by dividing the mean value of a given project characteristic by the mean number of project team members.

There could have been several reasons why the dollar amounts per person were larger for agile-driven software development projects than for plan-driven software development projects. Because agile-driven methods are at best 10 years old, whereas plan-driven methods are 20 or more years old, the information technology labor market could perceive that individuals who possess agile experience are more valuable than their plan-driven counterparts. In other words, ceteris paribus, the derived demand curve for individuals with agile-driven experience could be shifted to the right of the derived demand curve for individuals with plan-driven experience (Krugman & Wells, 2006). Although there was insufficient data collected in this study to conform or disconfirm this assertion, it is certainly worthy of additional research. Another reason for the positive difference could be that the dollar amounts for agile-driven software development projects were consistently underreported due to the turbulent and chaotic nature of agile-driven methodologies. Fleming and Koppleman (2000), Kerzner (2006), Meredith and Mantel (2003), and Schwalbe (2006) have all agreed that the costs of a software development project are poorly managed, and in an environment in flux, obtaining accurate budgeted or actual cost data may be difficult, if not impossible, to achieve. In any case, the collection of accurate data on dollars budgeted and dollars actually spent is yet another topic for further research.

Duration of the Projects. In this subsection of the analysis of the findings, the statistics on how long ago was a project completed, the estimated project duration, and the actual project duration are all examined one after the other. From Table 15, for known agile-driven plus probable agile-driven projects, the average number of months prior to a participant taking the survey was 3.8 months with a median of 2.3 months and a standard deviation of .9 months. From Table 16, for known plan-driven plus probable plan-driven projects, the average number of months prior to a participant taking the survey was 7.6 months with a median of 7.5 months and a standard deviation of 1.7 months. The coefficient of dispersion for agile-driven plus agile-driven projects was .237, whereas the coefficient of dispersion for known plan-driven plus probable plan-driven projects was .224. This means that in terms of the number of months prior to a respondent providing his or her data, the dispersion of the two data sets were approximately the same. A difference of means test was conducted out using the non-pooled t-test for two population means with unequal variances (Kutner et al., 2004). The value of the t-statistic was 16.894 with 44 degrees of freedom using the Welch-Satterthwaitte equation, and was statistically significant at the 99% confidence level (Satterthwaitte, 1946; Welch, 1947). In other words, in terms of the number of months prior to a participant taking the survey, the known agile-driven plus probable agile-driven projects were significantly different from the known plan-driven plus probable plan-driven projects.

The second concern to analyze is the estimated duration of the projects. From Table 15, for known agile-driven plus probable agile-driven projects, the average estimated duration was 7.0 months with a median of 6.1 months and a standard deviation of 2.2 months. From Table 16, for known plan-driven plus probable plan-driven projects, the average estimated duration was 8.4 months with a median of 7.7 months and a standard deviation of 2.4 months. The coefficient of dispersion for agile-driven plus agile-driven projects was .314, whereas the coefficient of dispersion for known plan-driven plus probable plan-driven projects was .286. This means that in terms of the estimated project duration, there was a slightly wider range of known agile-driven plus probable agile-driven projects than known plan-driven plus probable plan-driven projects. Again, a difference of means test was conducted out using the non-pooled t-test for two population means with unequal variances (Kutner et al., 2004). The value of the t-statistic was 3.914 with 38 degrees of freedom using the Welch-Satterthwaitte equation, and was statistically significant at the 99% confidence level (Satterthwaitte, 1946; Welch, 1947). In other words, in terms of the estimated duration of a project, the known agile-driven plus probable agile-driven projects were significantly different from the known plan-driven plus probable plan-driven projects.

The last topic to analyze is the actual duration of the projects. From Table 15, for known agile-driven plus probable agile-driven projects, the average actual duration was 7.9 months with a median of 7.1 months and a standard deviation of 2.5 months. From Table 16, for known plan-driven plus probable plan-driven projects, the average actual duration was 7.1 months with a median of 7.4 months and a standard deviation of 2.6 months. The coefficient of dispersion for agile-driven plus agile-driven projects was .316, whereas the coefficient of dispersion for known plan-driven plus probable plan-driven projects was .366. This means that in terms of the actual project duration, there was a slightly wider range of known plan-driven plus probable plan-driven projects than known agile-driven plus probable agile-driven projects. A third difference of means test was performed using the non-pooled t-test for two population means with unequal variances (Kutner et al., 2004). The value of the t-statistic was 2.140 with 41 degrees of freedom using the Welch-Satterthwaitte equation, and was statistically significant at the 95% confidence level, but statistically insignificant at the 99% confidence level (Satterthwaitte, 1946; Welch, 1947). In other words, in terms of the actual duration of a project, the known agile-driven plus probable agile-driven projects were not significantly different from the known plan-driven plus probable plan-driven projects.

The obvious problem with the mean actual duration of known agile-driven plus probable agile-driven projects of 7.9 months was that it is too long, given that the mean number of person hours expended is 2,303 person hours. Assuming that every individual in a project works 37.5 hours a week, there are 4.3 working weeks per month, and the average number of individuals in known agile-driven plus probable agile-driven projects is 7.9 project team members, the total number of person hours is 10,064 person hours, rounded to near hour. The ratio of the mean number of person hours expended for known agile-driven plus probable agile-driven projects to the maximum number of person hours that could be expended is .229 or 22.9%. There are two possibilities to examine; either project team members were concurrently working on multiple activities, or the number of person hours expended in known agile-driven plus probable agile-driven projects were systematically underreported by the participants. In contrast, because the mean number of individuals working on a known plan-driven or probable plan-driven project was 16.7 individuals, the maximum number of person hours is 19,119 person hours. The ratio of the mean number of person hours expended for known plan-driven plus probable plan-driven projects to the maximum number of person hours that could be expended is .276 or 27.6%. From a intuitive perspective, the two ratios differ by only .047, which is not a large number.

Furthermore, Cao (2006) found that the mean actual duration for a project using agile-driven methods was 9.9 months with median of 10.0 months and a standard deviation of 2.2 months. The coefficient of dispersion for the projects in Cao's (2006) study was .222, not much different from the coefficient of dispersion for actual duration of known agile-driven plus probable agile-driven projects in this study. A difference of means test was performed using the non-pooled t-test for two population means, where Cao's (2006) results were contrasted with the results from this study with unequal variances (Kutner et al., 2004). The value of the t-statistic was 6.424 with 85 degrees of freedom using the Welch-Satterthwaitte equation, and was statistically significant at the 99% confidence level. In other words, in terms of the actual duration of a project, there were indeed statistically significant differences between the results in Cao's (2006) study and this study. The implication is that there is evidence to suggest that the average actual duration of a known agile-driven plus probable agile-driven project found by this study is less than what was previously estimated. It may be that project team members are becoming more familiar with agile-driven methodologies, and thus agile-driven projects are experiencing production efficiencies (Krugman & Wells, 2006). This is clearly a topic for additional research. Unfortunately, no frequency data were found on the actual durations for plan-driven software development projects.

Characteristics of the Participants

The characteristics of the participants are broken up into two distinct categories. The first category deals with an individual's work life, such as his or her occupational classification, the number of years a respondent was engaged in that occupation, and the major role that a participant played in a project. The second category is concerned with a participant's personal features, such as his or her approximate and gender. The point of analyzing the characteristics of the participants along these lines is to see if there are statistically significant differences between participants involved in known agile-driven plus probable agile-driven projects and respondents who were part of known plan-driven plus probable plan-driven projects.

Table 52 *Major Roles for the Computer and Mathematical Occupations*

Major Roles Played	All Projects	Known Agile-Driven plus Probable Agile-Driven Projects	Known Plan-Driven plus Probable Plan-Driven Projects
	Count (Percent)	Count (Percent)	Count (Percent)
Project Directors	6 (9.5%)	5 (10.9%)	1 (5.9%)
Project Managers	21 (33.3%)	14 (30.4%)	7 (41.2%)
Project Team Members or Mangers	29 (46.1%)	23 (50.1%)	6 (35.2%)
Miscellaneous Roles	7 (11.1)	4 (8.6%)	3 (17.7%)
Total	63 (100.0%)	46 (100.0%)	17 (100.0%)

Work Related Issues. From Table 17, computer and mathematical occupations made up the largest group of participants, where 63 or 34.1% of the 185 respondents worked in these occupations. For known agile-driven plus probable agile-driven projects, 46 or 38.7% of the participants specified that he or she worked in computer or mathematical occupations, whereas for known plan-driven plus probable plan-driven projects, 17 or 25.8% of the participants reported that he or she was engaged in computer or mathematical occupations. From Table 19, 63 or 34.1% of the participants were either project team members or project team managers. This was strictly a coincidence, for when frequency reports were generated based on these subsets of the data, there was little commonality. Of the 63 participants who stated that he or she worked in computer or mathematical occupations, only 29 or 46.1% of these respondents were project team members or project team managers. Twenty-one or 33.3% of these 63 participants reported that he or she was engaged as a project manager and six or 9.5% were project directors. The remaining seven participants believed that he or she were customers, customer decision makers, customer representatives, or influencers. Table 52 contains the data.

Table 53 *Major Roles for Middle-Level and Senior-Level Managers*

Major Roles Played	All Projects	Known Agile-Driven plus Probable Agile-Driven Projects	Known Plan-Driven plus Probable Plan-Driven Projects
	Count (Percent)	Count (Percent)	Count (Percent)
Project Directors	19 (33.9%)	14 (39.0%)	5 (25.0%)
Project Managers	11 (19.6%)	8 (22.2%)	3 (15.0%)
Project Team Members or Mangers	12 (21.5%)	7 (19.4%)	5 (25.0%)
Miscellaneous Roles	14 (25.0%)	7 (19.4%)	7 (35.0%)
Total	56 (100.0%)	36 (100.0%)	20 (100.0%)

In Table 17, for all 185 data points, the next major occupational classification were middle-level managers with 34 participants followed by 22 senior-level managers, for a total of 56 participants who classified themselves as managers. Of these 56 participants, 36 individuals were involved in known agile-driven plus probable agile- driven projects, and 20 people worked in known plan-driven plus probable plan-driven projects. From Table 53, of these 56 middle-level and senior level managers, 19 were project directors, 11 were project managers, and 12 were project team members or managers. The remaining 14 participants were customers, customer decision makers, customer representatives, influencers, executive sponsors, or steering committee members.

When the business and financial occupations, the education, training, library, and museum occupations, the miscellaneous occupations, and the other occupations contained in Table 17 are compared to the major roles in Table 19, a more representative picture emerges, where data are portrayed in Table 54. In this case, there were a significant number of customer users, customer decision-makers, customer representatives as well as influencers. This was an important result because it meant that a large number of participants who classified themselves as customer users, customer decision-makers, customer representatives, influencers and the miscellaneous roles came from the business and financial occupations, the education, training, library, and museum occupations, the miscellaneous occupations, and the other occupations.

Table 54 *Major Roles for the Other Occupations Listed in Question 46*

Major Roles Played	All Projects	Known Agile-Driven plus Probable Agile-Driven Projects	Known Plan-Driven plus Probable Plan-Driven Projects
	Count (Percent)	Count (Percent)	Count (Percent)
Customer Users, Customer Decision-Makers, and Customer Representatives	8 (12.1%)	3 (8.1%)	5 (17.2%)
Influencers	7 (10.6%)	3 (8.1%)	4 (13.8%)
Project Directors	9 (13.6%)	6 (16.2%)	3 (10.3%)
Project Managers	13 (19.7%)	6 (16.2%)	7 (24.1%%)
Project Team Members or Mangers	22 (33.4%)	14 (37.8%)	8 (27.6%)
Miscellaneous Roles	7 (10.6%)	5 (13.6%)	3 (7.0%)
Total	66 (100.0%)	37 (100.0%)	20 (100.0%)

Another issue that is exposed by Tables 52, 53, and 54 is the relative dearth of actual customer data. According to Highsmith (2004), Poppendieck and Poppendieck (2006), and Schwaber (2004), in agile-driven projects, customers work side-by-side with the other team members. In other words, when an agile-driven project was completed, all of the project team members should possess a reasonably good idea of customer satisfaction, and thus the data from the various project team members could act as a proxy for data from actual customers. According to the agile-driven philosophy, project managers, project directors, and other project stakeholders should be intimately knowledgeable about customer satisfaction, and therefore, his or her data could act as a proxy for data from actual customers. Furthermore, Humphrey (1996), Humphrey (1999), Paulk et al. (1991), and Paulk et al. (1994) all agreed that customer satisfaction was definitely important, and should and ought to be the focus of the project team and the project management. Thus, it seems that the data from the different project stakeholders could again be used as a proxy for actual customer satisfaction data.

The remaining work related issue is the number of years that a participant was engaged in his or her occupation. From Table 22, for both known agile-driven plus probable agile-driven projects and known plan-driven plus probable plan-driven projects was 8.1 years. For known agile-driven plus probable agile-driven projects, the median was 8.7 years, whereas for plan-driven plus-probable plan-driven projects the median was 8.2 years. The standard deviations were .3 years for known agile-driven plus probable agile-driven projects and .2 years for known plan-driven plus probable plan-driven projects. The coefficients of dispersions were .037 for participants engaged in known agile-driven plus probable agile-driven projects and .025 years for respondents who worked in known plan-driven plus probable plan-driven projects. Furthermore, a difference of means test was conducted out using the non-pooled *t*-test for two population means with unequal variances (Kutner et al., 2004). The value of the *t*-statistic was .000 with 251 degrees of freedom using the Welch-Satterthwaitte equation, and was statistically insignificant at the 95% confidence level (Satterthwaitte, 1946; Welch, 1947). In other words, in terms of the number of years that a participant was engaged in an occupation, there was no statistically significant difference among the respondents.

Given the previous analysis on occupational classifications, the number of years a participant was engaged in an occupation, and the major roles played, it was apparent that the two populations were approximately homogeneous. This was an important result because it indicated that the significant issues that separate agile-driven and plan-driven methods could be the use and results of those software development methodologies, rather than the individuals who employed the methodologies.

Personal Issues. The participant personal issues are his or her approximate age and gender. From Table 22, the approximate age for all 185 respondents was 35.6 years, where the median age was 35.1 years and the standard deviation was 1.5 years. For known agile-driven plus probable agile-driven projects, the average approximate age was 34.8 years, where the median age was 34.6 years and the standard deviation was 1.3 years In contrast, for known plan-driven plus probable plan-driven projects, the average approximate age was 37.1 years, where the median age was 35.9 years and the standard deviation was 1.8 years. The coefficient of dispersion was .037 for participants who were involved in known agile-driven plus probable agile-driven projects and .049 for respondents who labored in known plan-driven plus probable plan-driven projects. This means that in terms of the approximate age of the participants, the breadth of the respondents who worked in project that employed agile-driven or plan-driven methods was about the same. A second difference of means test was calculated using the non-pooled *t*-test for two population means with unequal variances (Kutner et al., 2004). The value of the *t*-statistic was 9.142 with 46 degrees of freedom using the Welch-Satterthwaitte equation, and was statistically significant at the 99% confidence level (Satterthwaitte, 1946; Welch, 1947). In other words, in terms of the approximate age of the participants, the respondents who were involved in known agile-driven plus probable agile-driven projects were significantly younger than the respondents that were engaged in known plan-driven plus probable plan-driven projects.

As for the gender of the participants, it is apparent from Table 21 that there were no real differences between individuals who worked in known agile-driven plus probable agile-driven projects and individuals who worked in known plan-driven plus probable plan-driven projects. When considering all 185 participants, 155 were male and 30 were female, or 83.8% were male and 16.2% were female. For the known agile-driven plus probable agile-driven projects, 99 or 83.2% of the respondents were male and 20 or 16.8% of the respondents were female. For the known plan-driven plus probable plan-driven projects, 56 or 84.8% of the individuals were male and 10 or 15.2% of the individuals were female.

This is a surprising result, for Highsmith (2004), Poppendieck and Poppendieck (2006), and Schwaber (2004) all portrayed agile-driven methods as being egalitarian. The expectation of this researcher was that the percentage of females who were engaged in known agile-driven plus probable agile-driven projects would be greater than the percentage of females who were involved in known plan-driven plus probable plan-driven projects. Thus, an additional research topic is needed to explore why the percentages of males and females were approximately the same for both software development methodologies.

Thus, statistically significant differences appeared in the approximate ages of the participants, but not necessarily based on gender. Together with the conclusion that there were seemingly insignificant differences in the occupational classifications, the number of years that a respondent was engaged in an occupation, and the major role played in a project, it could be concluded that two participant populations differ only by age. In other words, the software development methodologies did matter, but not necessarily the individuals working in projects that employed those methodologies.

Potential Problems with a Project

From Table 23, of the 185 participants, 73 or 39.5% of the respondents recorded that no significant problems were encountered, where 38.8% of the known agile-driven plus probable agile-driven projects and 41.0% of the known plan-driven plus probable plan-driven project made that same statement. Thirty-two participants indicated that he or she came across significant problems that were not prescribed in question 42. Of these 32 participants,

21 provided data on known agile-driven plus probable agile-driven projects, and 11 furnished data on known plan-driven plus probable plan-driven projects. In Table 23, a number of pre-defined problems were grouped together to form a miscellaneous category, where 24 or 13.0% of the participants formed this grouping.

Of the possible responses to question 42, the most common response was that the project specifications were not clearly understood by the project team. For the known agile-driven plus probable agile-driven projects, 18 or 15.1% of the respondents made this selection, whereas for known plan-driven plus probable plan-driven projects, seven or 10.6% of the respondents made the same selection. This was a rather interesting result because Highsmith (2004), Poppendieck and Poppendieck (2006), and Schwaber (2004) univocally stated that in order for an agile-driven project to be successful, it required that the project team be highly trained, and highly motivated when compared to his or her counterparts in projects using plan-driven software development methodologies. The fact that the percentage was higher for known agile-driven plus probable agile-driven projects than the percentage for known plan-driven plus probable plan-driven projects seemed to indicate that agile project team members were not as high-powered as the agile literature seemed to imply. Thus, the output from this analysis was that additional research is needed to ascertain if this result is a fluke or an actual reflection of reality.

The apparent confusion regarding the use and results of the agile-driven software development methodology becomes apparent when examining the comments in Table 24. It seemed that many of the participants believed that the project team struggled not only to complete the project on budget and in a timely manner, but also grappled with the agile-driven software development methodology that was selected. In contrast, Table 25 lists some of the significant problems encountered by the project teams that were involved with plan-driven software development methodologies. For these individuals, the most significant problems dealt exclusively with bringing in the project on budget and on time, but not with the software development methodology that was chosen. In other words, the very newness of agile-driven methodologies could be the reason why some of the participants believed that the project team did not clearly understand the project specifications.

Finally, 15 or 8.1% of the respondents stated that the project team lacked knowledge of the company products and services. For the known agile-driven plus probable agile-driven projects, six of 5.0% of the participants believed the same way, whereas for known plan-driven plus probable plan-driven projects, nine or 13.6% of the participants felt likewise. This result was interesting because in percentage terms the number individuals engaged in known plan-driven plus probable plan-driven projects was more than double the percentage of individuals involved in known agile-driven plus probable agile-driven projects. This could be a strictly a random variation in the data, or it could be that project team members who worked in projects that employed plan-driven software development methodologies were less likely to understand the products and/or services of a firm. In any case, additional research is needed to understand better the result.

Regression Findings

The research question that propelled the study is: What is the difference, if any, in customer satisfaction between the use and results of agile-driven software development methods and the use and results of plan-driven software development software development methods? The results in this sub-section analyze the following hypotheses for known agile-driven plus probable agile-driven projects and known plan-driven plus probable plan-driven projects:

H0:   The autonomous customer satisfaction for a project using agile software development methods is equal to the autonomous customer satisfaction for a project using plan-driven software development methods.

$H1_a$:   The autonomous customer satisfaction for a project using agile software development methods is greater than the autonomous customer satisfaction for a project using plan-driven software development methods.

$H1_b$:   The autonomous customer satisfaction for a project using plan-driven software development methods is greater than the autonomous customer satisfaction for a project using agile software development methods.

The statistical procedure examined under what conditions could H0 and $H1_b$ be rejected at the 95% or 99% confidence levels. From Table 28 when the software development methodology was known, the constant term and the coefficients for product quality, project team effectiveness, and project management effectiveness were all statistically significant at the 99% confidence level. However, the coefficient for the dummy variable was positive and not statistically significant at the 95% confidence level. In other words, when the software development methodology was known, H0 cannot be rejected at the 95% confidence level. The dummy variable was removed, and Table 33 contains non-standardized estimates of the coefficients when the software development methodology was known by the respondents.

When the data from the participants who knew what software development methodology was employed was pooled with the data from the respondents who did not know what software development methodology was used, but the methodology was inferred, a slightly different picture emerges. From Table 38, the constant term and the coefficients for product quality, project team effectiveness, and project management effectiveness were all statistically significant at the 99% confidence level. However, the coefficient for the dummy variable was barely statistically significant at the 95% confidence level, but statistically insignificant at the 99% confidence level. It is argued in the succeeding paragraphs that the 99% confidence level was the appropriate confidence level rather than the 95% confidence level, because customer satisfaction, product quality, project team effectiveness, and project management effectiveness variables all contained averaged values. Given that the 99% confidence level was the appropriate confidence level to employ, Table 45 contains the values of the estimates for the coefficients when the dummy variable was removed from the regression equation.

Known Software Development Methodologies. When the participants knew the software development methodology employed, all of the coefficients in Table 29 were statistically significant at the 99% confidence level, except the coefficient for the dummy variable that was statistically insignificant at the 95% confidence level. From Table 27, the actual R-squared value was .681 and the adjusted R-squared value was .672, implying on an adjusted basis the regression explained 67.2% of the variance in customer satisfaction. Furthermore, from Table 28, the value of the F-statistic for the regression equaled 76.421 with four and 143 degrees of freedom, and was statistically significant at the 99% confidence level.

From Table 29, the non-standardized estimate of the constant term is 1.435 with a standard error of .499, a t-statistic value of 2.875, and a p-value of .005. In other words, the constant term is statistically significant at the 99% confidence level. Because the dummy variable is included in the model contained in Table 29, the constant term is interpreted as the level of autonomous customer satisfaction for known plan-driven plus probable plan-driven projects. If the coefficient of dummy variable had been statistically significant at the 95% confidence level, then coefficient of dummy variable is the contribution to autonomous customer satisfaction from employing agile-driven methods. On the other hand, because the coefficient of the dummy variable was not statistically significant at the 95% confidence level, the implication is that the constant term is interpreted to be the level of autonomous customer satisfaction regardless of the software development methodology employed.

The interpretation of the value of autonomous customer satisfaction requires clarification. Covey (1989) observed that only unsatisfied needs motivate human behavior, and thus prompt individuals, managers, and companies to develop software applications. In other words, if the needs of a customer were unsatisfied, it means that the value of customer satisfaction is probably between one and two. If the customer satisfaction variable equals one, then the customer is extremely dissatisfied, and if the value of the customer satisfaction variable equals two, then the customer is only dissatisfied. Thus, because the estimated value of the constant term equaled 1.435, it was apparent that the value of autonomous customer satisfaction appearing in Table 29 was consistent with Covey's (1989) statements.

From Table 29, the non-standardized estimate of the coefficient of the product quality variable was .443 with a standard error of .082, a t-statistic of 5.388 and a p-value equaling .000. In other words, the coefficient of product quality was statistically significant at the 99% confidence level. Hayes (1998) observed that the relevant software quality issues were correctness, reliability, usability, maintainability, testability, portability, inter-operability, intra-operability, and flexibility, and questions 19 through 25 addressed each one of these issues in turn except inter-operability, where it was argued previously that including the notion of inter-operability could introduce internal validity issues into the study. When correctness, reliability, usability, maintainability, testability, portability, intra-operability, and flexibility increase, the expectation was that product quality increased as well as customer satisfaction. This result was borne out because when assuming that a software application possessed the highest quality possible, then the value of the product quality variable equaled five on a 5-point Likert-type scale. When multiplying five by the non-standardized estimated value of the product quality coefficient, ceteris paribus, customer satisfaction increased by 2.215. Thus, the sign of the estimated coefficient of the product quality variable appeared to be correct.

Again from Table 29, the non-standardized estimate of the coefficient of the project team effectiveness variable was .473 with a standard error of .087, a t-statistic of 5.441 and a p-value equaling .000. Senge et al. (1994) observed that cross-functional teams permit teams coalesce, and Kouzes and Posner (1987) noticed that cross-functional teams encourage synergy by changing the leadership style from autocratic to participative in nature. Anderson (2004), Baheti et al. (2002), and Erdogmus (2003) all remarked that cross-functional teams formed the basis of agile-driven methods. Thus, the expectation was that the sign of the coefficient of the project team effectiveness variable is positive, and indeed it was positive. Furthermore, when a software development project team was working in an optimal fashion, the value of the project team effectiveness variable is five on a 5-point Likert-type scale. When five multiplied by the non-standardized estimate of the project team effectiveness coefficient, ceteris paribus, the increase in customer satisfaction was 2.365. In other words, project team effectiveness significantly contributed to customer satisfaction.

When restating the results from Table 29 for a third time, the non-standardized estimate of the coefficient of the project management effectiveness variable was -.357 with a standard error of .076, a *t*-statistic of -4.678 and a *p*-value equaling .000. On first glance, the sign of the non-standardized estimate of the coefficient of project team effectiveness appeared to be incorrect. However, Christensen (1997) argued that the reason projects fail was that the customary answers of planning better, working harder, and becoming more customer driven actually exacerbate the problem. One of the major goals of agile-driven methods was including customer input to ensure timely delivery of software products, whereas with plan-driven software development methodologies, the customer reviewed the progress at pre-established milestones or at the end of the project (Desaulniers & Anderson, 2001). In other words, the inter-workings of a software development project were the domain of the project manager and the project team, and not necessarily receiving customer input (Kerzner, 2006). Thus, the negative sign of the non-standardized estimate of the coefficient of the project management effectiveness variable makes sense. Finally, if the project management was performing optimally, the value of the project management effectiveness variable is five on a 5-point Likert-type scale, and the result was -1.785 when this maximal value is multiplied by the non-standardized estimate of the project management effectiveness coefficient. Thus, ceteris paribus, project management effectiveness significantly detracted from customer satisfaction.

Given that the non-standardized estimate of the coefficient of the dummy variable was statistically insignificant at the 95% confidence level, it was apparent that H0 cannot be rejected. The question that must be asked is why H0 cannot be rejected at the 95% confidence level. The answer appeared to come from the responses to question 16 that addressed project costs and from the responses to question 18 that dealt with project value. The counts and percentages of the responses to question 16 are contained in Table 55 and the counts and percentages of the responses to question 18 are shown in Table 56.

Table 55 *Cost of the Projects When Compared to the Cost of Other Projects Similar in Size When the Software Development Methodology Was Known*

Project Costs	All Projects	Known Agile-Driven Projects	Known Plan-Driven Projects
	Count (Percent)	Count (Percent)	Count (Percent)
Very Low Priced	8 (5.4%)	7 (7.4%)	1 (1.8%)
Low Priced	34 (23.0%)	24 (25.3%)	10 (18.9%)
About the Same	82 (55.4%)	49 (51.6%)	33 (62.3%)
High Priced	22 (14.9%)	13 (13.7%)	9 (17.0%)
Very High Priced	2 (1.3%)	2 (2.0%)	0 (0.0%)
Total	148 (100.0%)	95 (100.0%)	53 (100.0%)

When examining the data in Table 55, it is apparent that the participants believed that the project that he or she reported on was slightly lower priced than other projects of similar size. From previous analysis, the size of agile-driven projects were significantly different from plan-driven projects according to the number of person hours expected, the number of project team members, as well as the budgeted and actual dollars spent. When value of a software development project enters the picture, the results in Table 54 support the data in Table 55. For both known agile-driven projects and known plan-driven projects, customers and his or her proxies believed that the software development project that was reported cost less than projects of similar size, and was good to excellent value for the money that spent.

What questions 16 and 18 do not address is whether the results would be different if the participants were asked questions regarding cost and value, where the software development methodologies were different. In other words, if a participant had been involved in a plan-driven software development project, what would be the results if the comparison were with an agile-driven software development project, and vice versa? The answer to this question is an obvious topic for additional research.

The final piece of analysis in this subsection is concerned with concerned with the results in Table 34, where the software development methodology is known, but the dummy variable was removed. In this case, the constant term and all of the non-standardized estimates of the coefficients were statistically significant at the 99% confidence level. From Table 32, the actual R-squared value was .674 and the adjusted R-squared value was .667, implying on an adjusted basis the regression explained 66.7% of the variance in customer satisfaction. Furthermore, from Table 32, the value of the F-statistic for the regression equaled 99.071 with three and 144 degrees of freedom, and was statistically significant at the 99% confidence level. When these statistics were compared to the results in Tables 27 and 28, the findings are striking. The actual R-squared value declined by .007, whereas the adjusted R-squared value decreased by .005. However, the value of the F-statistic for the regression increased by 22.650. Thus, it appeared that when the software development methodology was known, the dummy variable was unnecessary. Furthermore, the non-standardized estimates of the constant term and the coefficients of the explanatory variables slightly increased, giving additional weight to the conclusion that H0 cannot be rejected at the 95% confidence level.

Table 56 *Description of the Projects in Terms of the Value for the Money When the Software Development Methodology Was Known*

Project Costs	All Projects	Known Agile-Driven Projects	Known Plan-Driven Projects
	Count (Percent)	Count (Percent)	Count (Percent)
Poor Value for the Money	12 (8.1%)	8 (8.4%)	4 (7.5%)
Fair Value	16 (10.8%)	6 (6.3%)	10 (18.9%)
Good Value	43 (29.1%)	28 (29.5%)	15 (28.3%)
Very Good Value	56 (37.8%)	41 (43.2%)	15 (28.3%)
Excellent Value for the Money	21 (14.2%)	12 (12.6%)	9 (17.0%)
Total	148 (100.0%)	95 (100.0%)	53 (100.0%)

Known versus Not Necessarily Known with the Dummy Variable. In the two remaining regressions, all 185 data points were used, where the known and probable software development methodologies were combined. From Table 40, all of the non-standardized estimates of the coefficients were statistically significant at the 99% confidence level, except the coefficient for the dummy variable that was barely statistically significant at the 95% confidence level. From Table 36, the actual R-squared value was .672 and the adjusted R-squared value was .665, meaning that on an adjusted basis the regression explained 66.5% of the variance in customer satisfaction. Furthermore, from Table 37, the value of the F-statistic equaled 92.121 with four and 180 degrees of freedom, and was statistically significant at the 99% confidence level.

From Table 40, the non-standardized estimate of the constant term was 1.233 with a standard error of .435, a t-statistic value of 2.832, and a p-value of .005. From Tables 28 and 38, when the software development methodology was not necessarily known and a dummy variable was included in the regression equation, the level of autonomous customer satisfaction for plan-driven projects declined by 14.1%. Using the information in Tables 28 and 38, a difference of means test was calculated for the two non-standardized estimates of the constant term using the pooled t-test for two population means with equal variances (Kutner et al., 2004). The value of the t-statistic was 3.943 with 331 degrees of freedom, and was statistically significant at the 99% confidence level. In other words, the mere knowledge of what specific plan-driven software development methodology was used had a positive effect on autonomous customer satisfaction.

From Table 40, the non-standardized estimate of the coefficient of the dummy variable was .165 with a standard error of .083, a t-statistic of 1.991, and a p-value of .048. The decline in autonomous customer satisfaction attributed to the use and results of agile-driven methods was therefore 4.1%. Again using the information in Tables 29 and 40, a difference of means test was calculated for the two non-standardized estimates of the coefficient for the dummy variable using the pooled t-test for two population means with equal variances (Kutner et al., 2004). The value of the t-statistic was .725 with 331 degrees of freedom, and was statistically insignificant at the 95% confidence level. Although the knowledge that an actual agile-driven software development methodology was employed also had a positive effect on autonomous customer satisfaction, this result meant that this knowledge was not statistically significant at the 95% confidence level.

The sign of the non-standardized estimate of the coefficient of the dummy variable also needs to be analyzed. Because the sign for the coefficient was positive rather than negative at the 95% confidence level, $H1_b$ can be rejected. In other words, at the 95% confidence level, it was rejected that the customer satisfaction for known plan-driven plus probable plan driven projects was greater than the customer satisfaction for known agile-driven plus probable agile-driven projects.

From Table 40, the non-standardized estimate for the coefficient for product quality was .474 with a standard error of .073, a t-statistic of 6.472, and a p-value of .000. Employing the information in Tables 29 and 40, a third difference of means test was calculated for the two non-standardized estimates of the coefficients of the product quality variable using the pooled t-test for two population means with equal variances (Kutner et al., 2004). The value of the t-statistic was 3.645 with 331 degrees of freedom, and was statistically significant at the 99% confidence level. In other words, when it was not necessarily known what software development methodology was employed, product quality was more important than when the software development methodology was known.

The non-standardized estimate for the coefficient for project team effectiveness from Table 40 was .461 with a standard error of .074, a t-statistic value of 6.240 and a p-value equal to .000. A fourth difference of means test was calculated using the information in Tables 29 and 40 for the two non-standardized estimates of the coefficients of the project team effectiveness variable employing the pooled t-test for two population means with equal variances (Kutner et al., 2004). The value of the t-statistic was 1.360 with 331 degrees of freedom, and was statistically insignificant at the 95% confidence level. In terms of project team effectiveness, this means that the knowledge of what software development methodology was employed did not significantly affect customer satisfaction.

The last variable to consider is project management effectiveness. From Table 40, the non-standardized estimate for the coefficient for project management effectiveness was -.314 with a standard error of .067, a t-statistic of -4.653, and a p-value of .000. From Tables 29 and 40, a fifth difference of means test was calculated for the two non-standardized estimates of the coefficients of the project management effectiveness variable using the pooled t-test for two population means with equal variances (Kutner et al., 2004). The value of the t-statistic was -5.099 with 331 degrees of freedom, and was statistically significant at the 99% confidence level. In other words, when the software development methodology was not necessarily known, the effective use of project management techniques had a statistically significant greater negative effect from when the software development methodology was known.

When the software development methodology was known, the non-standardized estimate of the coefficient of the dummy variable was statistically insignificant at the 95% confidence level. On the other hand, when software development methodology was not necessarily known, the non-standardized estimate of the coefficient of the dummy variable was barely statistically significant at the 95% confidence level, but statistically insignificant at the 99% confidence level. Thus, the question that needed to be asked was what is the appropriate level of statistical significance to use, 95% or 99%? Brace and Brace-Pellillo (2009) argued that "the correlation between two variables consisting of averages is usually higher than the correlation between two variables corresponding to actual raw data" (p. 522). Brace and Brace-Pellillo (2009) also suggested that it was appropriate to invoke a standard of cautiousness in the scientific, social science, and other scientific fields, and thus it made sense to use the low significance level of α equal to .01 when testing claims using averaged data. In other words, because customer satisfaction, product quality, project team effectiveness, and project management effectiveness variables all contained averaged values, the 99% confidence level was the more appropriate level of significance to use rather than the 95% confidence level. This means that the null hypothesis H0 could not rejected at the 99% confidence level.

Bonferroni (1935, 1936) further supported the idea that the 99% confidence level was the appropriate significance level to use. According to Bonferroni (1935, 1936), if a researcher is employing $k > 0$ explanatory variables on a data set, then the level of statistical significance to employ is $1/k$ times the desired level of statistical significance. In the four regression equations estimated in this study, there were either four or five variables, including the constant term. Thus, $1/k$ would either equal .25 or .20. By taking the minimum value of these two numbers, and then multiplying by α = .05, the Bonferroni (1935, 1936) correction procedure implies that the correct significance level is .01, again confirming that the 99% confidence level is the appropriate level of significance to employ.

The Bonferroni (1935, 1936) correction procedure is essentially a safeguard against the situation where multiple tests of statistical significance falsely indicate that significance exists when the level of significance occurred merely by chance. For example, if α = .05, then by chance one out of 20 tests for significance would point to a significant result when none existed. In other words, the Bonferroni (1935, 1936) correction procedure guards against reporting false positives by employing a stricter threshold for significance than what would normally be considered to be significant.

If the Brace and Brace-Pellillo (2009) and the Bonferroni (1935, 1936) positions are not accepted, and it is believed that the 95% confidence level is the confidence level to employ, consider the following additional arguments. First, from Table 40, at the 95% confidence level the confidence interval around the non-standardized estimate of the coefficient of the dummy variable was [.001, .329]. The lower bound of the lower of the confidence interval was nearly zero. In other words, it is possible that with a different data set, the lower bound of the confidence interval could be negative. Second, at the 95% confidence level, the percent increase in autonomous customer satisfaction is 13.4%, and from a qualitative perspective, it was not a large percent increase in autonomous customer satisfaction. Therefore, even if the 95% confidence level is accepted, the contribution to autonomous customer satisfaction when the agile-driven software development methodology was not necessarily known was not large.

Table 57 *Cost of the Projects When Compared to the Cost of Other Projects Similar in Size When the Software Development Methodology Was Known or Inferred*

Cost of the Projects	All Projects	Known Agile-Driven plus Probable Agile-Driven Projects	Known Plan-Driven plus Probable Plan-Driven Projects
	Count (Percent)	Count (Percent)	Count (Percent)
Very Low Priced	9 (4.9%)	7 (5.9%)	2 (3.0%)
Low Priced	45 (24.3%)	32 (26.9%)	13 (19.7%)
About the Same	96 (51.9%)	59 (49.6%)	37 (56.1%)
High Priced	30 (16.2%)	18 (15.1%)	12 (18.2%)
Very High Priced	5 (2.7%)	3 (2.5%)	2 (3.0%)
Total	185 (100.0%)	119 (100.0%)	66 (100.0%)

The reasons why the null hypothesis H0 cannot be rejected at the 99% confidence level are apparently the same, regardless of whether the software development methodology was known or not necessarily known. Table 57 contains the cost of the projects when compared to the cost of other projects similar in size when the software development methodology was not necessarily known. When comparing the data in Tables 57 and 58, it was apparent that the introduction of projects where the software development methodology was inferred did not modify the previous conclusion that the participants believed that the project that he or she reported on was slightly lower priced than similar projects. Furthermore, it was still correct to ask: If a participant was engaged in an agile-driven project, did the phrase "similar in size" mean other agile-driven projects or other plan-driven projects? The corresponding question that could be asked of participants that were involved in plan-driven projects is: If a participant was engaged in a plan-driven project, did the phrase "similar in size" mean other plan-driven projects or other agile-driven projects?

When the counts and percentages for question 18 contained in Table 58 are analyzed, again the conclusion seems to be the same. For the185 respondents, regardless of what software development methodology was used, he or she believed that the customers felt that the projects under scrutiny were a good to excellent value for the money. Thus, the pooling of projects where the software development methodology was known with the software development projects where the software development methodology was inferred does not appear to modify the content of the additional research question.

Table 58 *Description of the Projects in Terms of the Value for the Money When the Software Development Methodology Was Known or Inferred*

Value of the Projects	All Projects	Known Agile-Driven plus Probable Agile-Driven Projects	Known Plan-Driven plus Probable Plan-Driven Projects
	Count (Percent)	Count (Percent)	Count (Percent)
Poor Value for the Money	15 (8.1%)	9 (7.6%)	6 (9.0%)
Fair Value	23 (12.4%)	10 (8.4%)	13 (19.7%)
Good Value	58 (31.4%)	38 (31.9%)	20 (30.3%)
Very Good Value	65 (35.1%)	48 (40.3%)	17 (25.8%)
Excellent Value for the Money	24 (13.0%)	14 (11.8%)	10 (15.2%)
Total	185 (100.0%)	119 (100.0%)	66 (100.0%)

Known versus Not Necessarily Known without the Dummy Variable. The final regression equation to be analyzed is contained in Table 45, where the dummy variable was not included. In this case, the constant term and all of the non-standardized estimates of the coefficients were statistically significant at the 99% confidence level. From Table 43, the actual R-squared value was .665 and the adjusted R-squared value was .659, or on an adjusted basis, the regression explained 65.9% of the variance in customer satisfaction. Furthermore, from Table 44, the value of the F-statistic for the regression equaled 119.550 with three and 181 degrees of freedom, and was statistically significant at the 99% confidence level. When these statistics were compared to the results in Tables 38 and 39, the findings are remarkable. The actual R-squared value declined by .007, whereas the adjusted R-squared value decreased by .006. However, the value of the F-statistic for the regression increased by 27.429. Thus, it seems that employing an α equal to .01 was appropriate, and the null hypothesis H0 cannot be rejected at the 99% confidence level.

From Table 45, the non-standardized estimate of the constant term was 1.251 with a standard error or .439, a t-statistic value of 2.853, and a p-value of .005. Using the information in Tables 34 and 45, a difference of means test was calculated for the two non-standardized estimates of the constant term using the pooled t-test for two population means with equal variances (Kutner et al., 2004). The value of the t-statistic was 3.677 with 331 degrees of freedom, and was statistically significant at the 99% confidence level. In other words, the knowledge of what specific software development methodology was used had a positive effect on autonomous customer satisfaction, regardless of what methodology was employed.

From Table 45, the non-standardized estimate for the coefficient for product quality was .492 with a standard error of .073, a t-statistic of 6.734, and a p-value of .000. Employing the information in Tables 34 and 45, a second difference of means test was calculated for the two non-standardized estimates of the coefficients of the product quality variable using the pooled t-test for two population means with equal variances (Kutner et al., 2004). The value of the t-statistic was 3.762 with 331 degrees of freedom, and was statistically significant at the 99% confidence level. In other words, when it was not necessarily known what software development methodology was employed, product quality was again more important than when the software development methodology was known.

The non-standardized estimate for the coefficient for project team effectiveness from Table 45 was .465 with a standard error or .074, a t-statistic value of 6.254 and a p-value equal to .000. A third difference of means test was calculated using the information in Tables 33 and 43 for the two non-standardized estimates of the coefficients of the project team effectiveness variable employing the pooled t-test for two population means with equal variances (Kutner et al., 2004). The value of the t-statistic was 2.039 with 331 degrees of freedom, and was statistically significant at the 95% confidence level, but statistically insignificant at the 99% confidence level. If the 95% confidence level was the acceptable confidence level, then in terms of project team effectiveness, this result meant that the knowledge of the software development methodology employed provided significantly greater customer satisfaction than if the software development methodology was not necessarily known. On the other hand, if the arguments by Brace and Brace-Pellillo (2009) and Bonferroni (1935, 1936) positions were accepted, and the 99% confidence level was accepted, then in terms of project team effectiveness, the result implied that the knowledge of what software development methodology was used did not significantly affect customer satisfaction.

The last variable to consider is project management effectiveness. From Table 45, the non-standardized estimate for the coefficient for project management effectiveness was -.311

with a standard error of .068, a t-statistic of -4.574, and a p-value of .000. From Tables 34 and 45, a fourth difference of means test was calculated for the two non-standardized estimates of the coefficients of the project management effectiveness variable using the pooled t-test for two population means with equal variances (Kutner et al., 2004). The value of the t-statistic was -5.188 with 331 degrees of freedom, and was statistically significant at the 99% confidence level. In other words, when the software development methodology was not necessarily known, the effective use of project management techniques had a statistically significant greater negative effect from when the software development methodology was known.

Some Comments from the Participants

From Table 48, 134 or 72.4% of the 185 participants did not provide any additional comments. For the respondents that engaged in known agile-driven plus probable agile-driven projects, 86 individuals decided not to enter comments, whereas 48 of the respondents that were involved in known plan-driven plus probable plan-driven projects behaved in the same manner. In contrast, 51 of the 185 participants did provide additional comments, where 33 individuals reported on known agile-driven plus probable agile-driven projects and 18 individuals transmitted data on known plan-driven plus probable plan-driven projects. Thus, slightly over a quarter of the participants communicated additional comments, regardless of the software development methodology employed.

Known Agile-Driven plus Probable Agile-Driven Projects. For the participants that were engaged in known agile-driven plus probable agile-driven projects, two classes of comments were provided, the first class dealt with the particular software development methodology employed, whereas the second class was concerned with the software project itself. This result was similar to the result that was found when the responses to the most significant problem question was previously analyzed. Question 51 of the survey in Appendix C appeared to be another vehicle for a participant to criticize the workings of an agile-driven software development project. Thus, the remarks of the respondents in question 51 provided even more reasons why additional research is needed to reveal the problems that can and do occur when an agile-driven software development methodology is used.

Known Plan-Driven plus Probable Plan-Driven Projects. Of the 18 participants who wrote additional comments for the known plan-driven plus probable plan-driven projects, almost all of the statements were concerned with the projects themselves, or with the environment in which a project existed. None of the statements criticized the specific plan-driven software development methodology that was employed. The comments from these participants seemed to confirm that additional research is needed to reveal why agile-driven software development methodologies were a source of concern for the participants, whereas the respondents ignored the plan-driven software development methodologies.

Summary

In this section, the findings and the analysis of the findings are summarized. First, the various software development methodologies associated with the projects were discussed, followed by a depiction of the characteristics of the projects and a description of the characteristics of the participants. Next, the results of the four regression equations were reviewed in terms of the software development methodology that was employed. Finally, when the four regression equations were paired on the basis of whether the software development methodology was known to the participants of the study or whether the software development methodology was not necessarily known, the results of the difference of means tests is outlined.

Table 59 *Summary of the Results for the Characteristics of the Projects*

Characteristics of the Projects	Known Agile-Driven plus Probable Agile-Driven Projects versus Known Plan-Driven plus Probable Plan-Driven Projects
Number of Person Hours Expended	Statistically significant difference**
Number of Project Team Members	Statistically significant difference**
Budgeted Dollar Amounts	Statistically significant difference**
How Long Ago Was the Project Completed	Statistically significant difference**
Estimated Project Durations	Statistically significant difference**
Actual Project Durations	Statistically significant difference*

Note. A single asterisk indicates that the statistical significance was at the 95% confidence level, and a double asterisk specifies that the statistical significance was at the 99% confidence level.

The study contained 95 known agile-driven projects, 53 known plan-driven projects, and 37 software development projects where the participant did not know what software development methodology was employed. When the software development methodology was in question, a series of three questions were asked of each participant, inquiring about the project characterization, the project environment, and the project management. A majority rule was invoked, and it was inferred that 24 projects were probably agile-driven and 13 projects were probably plan-driven. Two Chow (1960) tests were conducted to see if the known agile-driven projects could be pooled with the probable agile-driven projects, and the known plan-driven projects could be combined with the probable plan-driven projects. The two Chow (1960) tests were statistically insignificant at the 95% confidence level, indicating that the pooling process was entirely appropriate to do.

Frequencies distributions for number of person hours expended, the number of project team members, the budgeted dollar amounts, the length of from when a project was completed, the estimated project durations, and the actual project durations were presented. The means, medians, and standard deviations were also calculated. When the characteristics of the known agile-driven plus probable agile-driven projects were compared with the characteristics of the known plan-driven plus probable plan-driven projects via six difference of means tests, the results are contained in Table 59. The difference of means tests assumed that the variances were not equal.

Five of the six difference of means tests were statistically significant at the 99% confidence level, where the difference of means test for the actual duration of the projects was only statistically significant at the 95% confidence level. Essentially, this result implied that the structure of the known agile-driven plus probable agile-driven projects was consistent with conventional wisdom regarding agile-driven projects (Chin, 2004; Highsmith, 2004; Schwaber, 2004). Furthermore, the mean number of project team members and the average project duration was compared using a difference of means test with the results obtained by Cao (2006). For the number of project team members, the average calculated in this study (i.e., 7.9 individuals) was statistically insignificant at the 95% confidence level from the average found in Cao's (2006) study (i.e., 8.4 individuals). When the means of actual project durations from two studies were compared using difference of means test, the average actual duration for the known agile-driven plus probable agile-driven projects in this study was significantly smaller at the 95% confidence level from the mean actual duration found in Cao's (2006) study. Unfortunately, no frequency data were found on the number of project team members and actual durations for plan-driven software development projects.

Table 60 *Summary of the Results for the Characteristics of the Participants*

Characteristics of the Participants	Known Agile-Driven plus Probable Agile-Driven Projects versus Known Plan-Driven plus Probable Plan-Driven Projects
Occupational Classification	Apparent homogeneous distribution
Years in the Selected Occupation	Statistically insignificant difference
Major Role Played	Apparent homogeneous distribution
Approximate Age	Statistically significant difference**
Gender	Apparent homogeneous distribution

Note. A single asterisk indicates that the statistical significance was at the 95% confidence level, and a double asterisk specifies that the statistical significance was at the 99% confidence level.

When the characteristics of the participants are examined, Table 60 shows that the participants were homogeneous regardless of the software development methodology that was employed, except that the approximate age of the respondents that were engaged in known plan-driven plus probable plan-driven projects was significantly higher than the respondents who were involved in known agile-driven plus probable agile-driven projects. The result for the approximate age of the participants was expected, because plan-driven software development methodologies are ten to 20 years older than agile-driven software development methodologies. The results in Tables 59 together with the results in Table 60 seemed to indicate that the 185 participants were a representative sample of his or her respective software development methodologies.

When the most significant problem encountered was examined, the most common problem experienced was that the project team members did not clearly understand the project specifications. In fact, in percentage terms, about 5% more of the project teams that engaged in known agile-driven plus probable agile-driven projects failed to understand the project specifications when compared to the project team members that were involved in known plan-driven plus probable plan-driven projects. This could have meant that agile-driven methods are less understood than plan-driven methods.

Table 61 contains the results of the two regressions that included a dummy variable representing the contribution to autonomous customer satisfaction. In the first entry, the results are for the regression when only known agile-driven and known plan-driven data were employed. In this case, the constant term, and the non-standardized estimates of the coefficients for product quality, project team effectiveness, and project management effectiveness were all statistically significant at the 99% confidence level. However, the non-standardized estimate of the coefficient for the dummy variable was statistically insignificant at the 95% confidence level, indicating that if the software development methodology was known, there was no difference in autonomous customer satisfaction. In other words, when the software development methodology was known, the null hypothesis H0 cannot be rejected at the 95% confidence level.

Table 61 *Summary of the Results for the Regressions with the Dummy Variable*

Regression Equations with the Dummy Variable Included	Statistical Results of the Regressions
Known Agile-Driven Projects and Known Plan-Driven Projects	The constant term and the non-standardized estimates of the coefficients of the explanatory variables were statistically significant at the 99% confidence level. The non-standardized coefficient of the dummy variable was statistically insignificant at the 95% confidence level.
Known Agile-Driven plus Probable Agile-Driven Projects and Known Plan-Driven plus Probable Plan-driven Projects	The constant term and the non-standardized estimates of the coefficients of the explanatory variables were statistically significant at the 99% confidence level. The non-standardized coefficient of the dummy variable was statistically significant at the 95% confidence level, but statistically insignificant at the 99% confidence level.

Note. The explanatory variables were product quality, project team effectiveness, and project management effectiveness. The dummy variable equaled zero for known plan-driven plus probable plan-driven projects and one for known agile-driven plus probable agile-driven projects.

In the second entry in Table 61, the results are summarized from the regression equation when all 185 data points are employed. In this case, the dummy variable equaled zero for the known plan-driven plus probable plan-driven projects and equaled one for the known plan-driven plus probable plan driven projects. The non-standardized estimates for all of the coefficients were statistically significant at the 99% confidence level, except the non-standardized estimate for the coefficient of the dummy variable. It was barely statistically significant at the 95% confidence level. Brace and Brace-Pellillo (2009) and Bonferroni (1935, 1936) both suggested that the 99% confidence level was the more appropriate level of significance to employ because customer satisfaction and the other explanatory variables contained averaged data. Thus, even in this case, if the Brace and Brace-Pellillo (2009) and Bonferroni (1935, 1936) arguments are accepted, the contribution made by the known agile-driven plus probable agile-driven projects to autonomous customer satisfaction is statistically insignificant. In other word, the null hypothesis H0 cannot be rejected at the 99% confidence level.

When the dummy variable was removed from the regression equation, Table 62 shows that the results were essentially the same, regardless of whether known agile-driven and known plan-driven data were employed, or known agile-driven plus probable agile-driven and known plan-driven plus probable plan-driven data were used. The constant term and the non-standardized estimates of the coefficients of product quality, project team effectiveness, and project management effectiveness were all statistically significant at the 99% confidence level. Given that there was only a minor reduction in the adjusted R-squared values, it appeared that the use of a dummy variable to represent the contribution to autonomous customer satisfaction in the use and results of agile-driven methods was not necessary.

Table 62 *Summary of the Results for the Regressions without the Dummy Variable*

Regression Equations without the Dummy Variable Included	Statistical Results of the Regressions
Known Agile-Driven Projects and Known Plan-Driven Projects	The constant term and the non-standardized estimates of the coefficients of the explanatory variables were statistically significant at the 99% confidence level.
Known Agile-Driven plus Probable Agile-Driven Projects and Known Plan-Driven plus Probable Plan-Driven Projects	The constant term and the non-standardized estimates of the coefficients of the explanatory variables were statistically significant at the 99% confidence level.

Note. The explanatory variables were product quality, project team effectiveness, and project management effectiveness.

When a series of difference of means tests were conducted on the two regression equations that contained a dummy variable, the results are displayed in Table 63. For the constant term and the non-standardized estimates of the coefficients for product quality and project management effectiveness, the difference of the means t-statistics were statistically significant at the 99% confidence level. In other words, the constant term or the level of autonomous customer satisfactions was significantly higher when the software development methodology was known. Furthermore the non-standardized estimates of the coefficients for product quality and project management effectiveness were significantly smaller when the software development methodology was known. In terms of product quality, this means that product quality was less of an issue when the software development methodology was known. As for project management effectiveness, when the software development methodology was known, an effective use of project management techniques had less of a negative effect on customer satisfaction when the project management technique was not necessarily known.

Table 63 *Summary of the Difference of Means Tests When the Dummy Variable Was Present in the Regression Equations*

Explanatory Variables	Known Agile-Driven and Known Plan-Driven Projects versus Known Agile-Driven plus Probable Agile-Driven Projects and Known Plan-Driven plus Probable Plan-Driven Projects
(Constant)	Statistically significant difference**
Dummy Variable	Statistically insignificant difference
Product Quality	Statistically significant difference**
Project Team Effectiveness	Statistically insignificant difference
Project Management Effectiveness	Statistically significant difference**

Note. The Dummy Variable equaled zero for plan-driven projects and one for agile-driven projects.
Note. A single asterisk indicates that the statistical significance was at the 95% confidence level, and a double asterisk specifies that the statistical significance was at the 99% confidence level.

When the dummy variable was removed from the regression equation, Table 64 records the difference of the means t-statistics for the constant term and the non-standardized estimates of the coefficients for the three explanatory variables. All of the t-statistics were statistically significant at the 99% confidence level, except the t-statistic associated with project team effectiveness which was statistically significant at the 95% confidence level. In other words, for the constant term, when the software development methodology was known, the constant term, or the level of autonomous customer satisfaction was significantly larger than when the software development methodology was not necessarily known. For product quality and project management effectiveness, the non-standardized estimates of the coefficients were significantly smaller when the software development methodology was known. This means that product quality was more important when the software development methodology was not known than when it was known. For project management effectiveness, the variable had less of a negative effect on customer satisfaction when the software development methodology was not necessarily known than when it was known. As for project team effectiveness, at the 95% confidence level, this variable had a statistically less of a significant effect when the software development methodology was not necessarily known than when it was known. If the Brace and Brace-Pellillo (2006) and Bonferroni (1935, 1936) arguments are accepted and 99% confidence level is indeed the appropriate level of significance to employ, then there was no statistically significant difference in the non-standardized estimates of the coefficients for project team effectiveness. In other words, result was the same as when the regression contained the dummy variable, and the knowledge of the software development methodology used did not significantly affect the level of customer satisfaction from the perspective of project team effectiveness.

Table 64 *Summary of the Difference of Means Tests When the Dummy Variable Was Not Present in the Regression Equations*

Explanatory Variables	Known Agile-Driven and Known Plan-Driven Projects versus Known Agile-Driven plus Probable Agile-Driven Projects and Known Plan-Driven plus Probable Plan-Driven Projects
(Constant)	Statistically significant difference**
Product Quality	Statistically significant difference**
Project Team Effectiveness	Statistically significant difference*
Project Management Effectiveness	Statistically significant difference**

Note. A single asterisk indicates that the statistical significance was at the 95% confidence level, and a double asterisk specifies that the statistical significance was at the 99% confidence level.

CHAPTER 5 – SUMMARY, CONCLUSIONS, AND RECOMMENDATIONS

Summary

Overview

The purpose of this study was to examine the relationship between customer satisfaction and the use and results of agile-driven software development methods as well as plan-driven software development methods. The goal of the study was to identify the relationship between customer satisfaction and product quality, project team effectiveness, and project management effectiveness, and determine if the use and results of agile-driven software development methods had an increased effect on customer satisfaction over and above the use and results of plan-driven software development methods.

This study attempted to examine empirically the first principle of the *Agile Manifesto*, where it was stated that customer satisfaction is of the highest priority, and is achieved through the rapid and continuous deliver if useful and valuable software (Beck, et al., 2001). The study focused on the question: What is the difference, if any, in customer satisfaction between the use and results of agile-driven software development methods and the use and results of plan-driven software development software development methods? If there is a difference, then the use and results of agile-driven software development methods could be viewed as superior to the use and results of plan-driven software development methods. If not, then other studies would need to be conducted to answer the question either affirmatively or negatively.

The study discussed the characteristics of the various agile-driven and plan-driven software development methods. Agile-driven methods were defined as being lightweight in the sense that short iterative cycles are employed to establish, prioritize, and verify requirements, where tacit knowledge of team members is substituted for documentation (Boehm & Turner, 2004). The types of agile-driven methods that were outlined included Extreme Programming, Adaptive Software Development, Crystal Methods, Scrum, Feature Driven Development, Dynamic Systems Development, and Lean Development. Plan-driven methods were considered to be traditional software development methods, where the approach to software development came from mainline engineering fields that employed the requirement/design/build paradigm, and focused on continuous improvement (Boehm & Turner, 2004). The types of plan-driven methods that were discussed included a variety of military standards, the ISO, EIA, and IEE standards, Software Factory, Cleanroom

Methodology, Capability Maturity Model, Capability Maturity Model Integration, Personal Software Process, and Team Software Process.

Literature Review

The literature regarding customer satisfaction, product quality, project team effectiveness, and project management effectiveness was then reviewed. Anderson (2004) and Highsmith (2004) stated individuals and interactions were more valuable to the success of a software development project than processes and tools. Engle and Blackwell (1982) and Vavra (1007) agreed that customer satisfaction was essential in project development, whereas Kan (1995) noticed that customer satisfaction was one of the major goals of Total Quality, a precursor to both agile-driven and plan-driven software development methods. McCall (1979) and MacMillan and Vosburgh (1986) discussed the importance of product quality, whereas Hayes (1998) attempted to characterize product quality in terms of correctness, reliability, usability, maintainability, testability, portability, inter-operability, and intra-operability. Senge et al. (1994) and Anderson (2004) stressed the importance of cross-functional teams as a basis for project team effectiveness. Finally, Kerzner (2006) argued that project management effectiveness was measured by the ability to complete a project in a timely manner and approximately on budget.

Methodology

The null hypothesis H0 and the two alternative hypotheses $H1_a$ and $H1_b$ were restated. The null hypothesis H0 asserted that the level of autonomous customer for agile-driven software development projects was the same as the level of autonomous customer satisfaction for plan-driven software development projects. The first alternative hypothesis $H1_a$ stated that the level of autonomous customer for agile-driven software development projects was greater than the level of autonomous customer satisfaction for plan-driven software development projects. The second alternative hypothesis $H1_b$ maintained that the level of autonomous customer for agile-driven software development projects was less than the level of autonomous customer satisfaction for plan-driven software development projects.

There was a short discussion on the pre-test/post-test research strategy and the post-test only methodology. It was decided for practical reasons that the post-test only research strategy was the more viable strategy to employ in this study. The different sections of the survey were examined in detail, including the questions on project information, customer satisfaction, product quality, project team effectiveness, project management effectiveness, most significant problem encountered, demographic information on a respondent, and a short section thanking an individual for his or her participation. The selection of the participants was described, where it was decided that posting the letter in Appendix B on the Yahoo.com and Google.com would attract a number of people to participate in the study. Furthermore, the various SPIN organizations affiliated with the Software Engineering Institute were contacted in the hope of collecting data on the plan-driven software development methodologies. The SurveyGold software package was discussed, outlining how it worked, from collecting the data, transferring the data to this researcher's computer in a secure manner, and providing a preliminary analysis.

Findings

The study empirically examined data from 185 software development projects, of which 95 were known agile-driven projects, 24 were probably agile-driven projects, 53 were known plan-driven projects, and 13 were probably plan-driven projects. The importance of analyzing the characteristics of the projects was provided. At the 95% confidence level, it was not possible to reject the null hypothesis when using data from known agile-driven and known plan-driven software development projects. Furthermore, when all of the data were employed, it was possible to reject the null hypothesis H0 at the 95% confidence level, but not at the 99% confidence level, which turned out to be the more appropriate level of significance to use (Brace & Brace-Pellillo, 2009; Bonferroni, 1935, 1936). Without a careful analysis of the project characteristics, it was decided that the agile-driven community could reject the results of this study if it was believed that the data were not representative of agile-driven software development projects (Chin, 2004; Highsmith, 2004; Schwaber, 2004). Because a number of questions were asked to characterize customer satisfaction, product quality, project team effectiveness, and project management effectiveness, Cronbach's alpha values were calculated when the software development methodology was known, when the software development methodology was inferred, and when the two were appropriately combined. For customer satisfaction, questions 12, 15, 16, and 17 were removed in order to achieve the highest possible Cronbach's alpha values. In contrast, for product quality, project team effectiveness, and project management effectiveness, there was no need to remove any question when calculating the highest possible Cronbach's alpha values. The 5-point Likert-type values for the questions were then averaged, forming the values for the dependent and explanatory variables for each data point.

The regression equation was stated, where customer satisfaction was dependent variable, and product quality, project team effectiveness, and project management effectiveness were the explanatory variables. The issues of heteroscedasticity, autocorrelation, and multicollinearity were discussed in some detail. The strengths and weaknesses of the study were explained, particularly in terms of confounding, reliability, and validity. The various ethical issues were reviewed, including the notions of informed consent, beneficence and non-malfeasance, justice, trust, fidelity to science, and potential ethical conflicts. Of the various ethical issues reviewed, it was believed that informed consent was critical, and needed to be emphasized in the questionnaire.

The frequency results for the various software development projects that were provided by the participants were reported. Essentially, there were 95 known agile-driven projects, 53 known plan-driven projects, and 37 projects where a participant did not know what software development methodology was employed. For these 37 participants, a series of three questions were asked of each respondent regarding the project characterization, project environment, and project management. Using the principle of majority rule, it was inferred that 24 projects were probably agile-driven and 13 projects were probably plan-driven. Two Chow (1960) tests were then conducted, and it was determined at the 95% confidence level that there were no statistically significant differences between known agile-driven projects and inferred or probable agile-driven projects. Furthermore, it was also established at the 95% confidence level that there were no statistically significant differences between known plan-driven projects and inferred or probable plan-driven projects. In other words, the known agile-driven projects could be pooled with the probable agile-driven projects, and the known plan-driven projects could be combined with the probable plan-driven projects.

The study presented the frequency results for the characteristics of the projects, including the number of person hours expended, the number of project team members, the budgeted dollar amounts for a project, how long ago the project was completed, the estimated duration of a project, and the actual duration of a project. Because the underlying measurements of the project characteristics were continuous, their means, medians, and standard deviations were calculated. The study also exhibited the frequency results for the characteristics of the participants, including a respondent's occupational classification, how long he or she had been engaged in that occupation, the major role played by a participant in the project under consideration, the approximate age of a respondent, and the gender of a respondent. Because the underlying measurement for the number of years a respondent was engaged in his or her selected occupation and because the approximate age of a respondent were both continuous variables, their means, medians, and standard deviations were also computed.

The data regarding the most significant problem encountered by a participant were then analyzed. For the 185 participants, 73 encountered no significant problems. Of these 73 individuals, 46 worked in known agile-driven plus probable agile-driven projects, and 27 labored in known plan-driven plus probable plan-driven projects. Twenty-five respondents stated that the major problem encountered was that the project team did not clearly understand the project specifications. Of these 25 participants, 18 were involved in known agile-driven plus probable agile-driven projects, and seven were connected to known plan-driven plus probable plan-driven projects. In other words, in 15.1% of the known agile-driven plus probable agile-driven projects, the project team members did not understand the project specifications, whereas in 10.6% of the known plan-driven plus probable plan-driven projects, the project team members encountered the same problem. The remaining 87 participants recorded a large range of significant problems, some of which were listed in question 42, whereas other problems were identified by the respondents, but not listed in question 42.

The results of estimating the non-standardized coefficients of four regression equations were examined. The first regression used only known agile-driven and known plan-driven project data, where a dummy variable was included among the explanatory variables. The dummy variable equaled zero for known plan-driven projects and equaled one for known agile-driven projects. The adjusted R-squared value was .672 and the F-statistic for the regression with four and 143 degrees of freedom was statistically significant at the 99% confidence level. All of the estimates of the non-standardized coefficients for the explanatory variables, including the constant term, were statistically significant at the 99% confidence level. However, the estimate of the non-standardized coefficient for the dummy variable was statistically insignificant at the 95% confidence level. A second regression equation was presented, using only known agile-driven and known plan-driven data, but without a dummy variable included among the explanatory variables. The adjusted R-squared value was .667 and the F-statistic for the regression with three and 144 degrees of freedom was statistically significant at the 99% confidence level. All of the estimates of the non-standardized coefficients for the explanatory variables were statistically significant at the 99% confidence level.

All 185 data points were used to estimate the values of the non-standardized coefficients in the third regression. Again, a dummy variable was included as an explanatory variable, where the dummy variable equaled zero for known plan-driven plus probable plan-driven projects and equaled one for known agile-driven plus probable agile-driven projects. The adjusted R-squared value was .665 and the F-statistic for the regression with four and

180 degrees of freedom was statistically significant at the 99% confidence level. All of the estimates of the non-standardized coefficients for the explanatory variables, including the constant term, were statistically significant at the 99% confidence level. However, the estimate of the non-standardized coefficient for the dummy variable was barely statistically significant at the 95% confidence level, but statistically insignificant at the 99% confidence level. Because it was thought that the 99% confidence level was more appropriate, a fourth regression equation was calculated, where dummy variable was excluded from the list of explanatory variables. In this case, the adjusted R-squared value was .659 and the F-statistic for the regression with three and 181 degrees of freedom was statistically significant at the 99% confidence level. All of the estimates of the non-standardized coefficients for the explanatory variables, including the constant term, were statistically significant at the 99% confidence level.

In presenting the findings of the study, the additional comments were outlined. Of the 185 respondents, only 51 provided additional comments. The percentages of individuals who gave additional comments was approximately 28%, and did not vary depending on the software development methodology that was known or inferred. For the projects that used agile-driven methods or were inferred to have used agile-driven methods, the participants commented on project characteristics and on the agile-driven methodology employed. For the projects that used plan-driven methods or were inferred to have used plan-driven methods, the participants commented only on the project characteristics and not on the plan-driven methodology used. When analyzing the comments, it appeared that the participants were more comfortable with plan-driven software development methods than he or she was with agile-driven software development methods. This situation was attributed to the relative newness of the agile-driven methodologies.

Analysis of the Findings

When analyzing the findings, several interesting issues were discovered. In terms of the number person hours expended, at the 99% confidence level, known agile-driven plus probable agile-driven projects were significantly smaller than known plan-driven plus probable plan-driven projects. In terms of the number of individuals in a project team, at the 99% confidence level, known agile-driven plus probable agile-driven projects were also significantly smaller than known plan-driven plus probable plan-driven projects. The mean number of project team members for known agile-driven plus probable agile-driven projects was 7.9 individuals, and the average number individuals engaged in known plan-driven plus probable plan-driven projects was 16.7 individuals. Because the two numbers were so different, the mean number of project team members found by Cao (2006) was compared to the average number of project teams involved with known agile-driven plus probable agile-driven projects using a difference of means test. The results were insignificant at the 95% confidence level, implying that the mean number of project team members for agile-driven plus probable agile-driven projects was reasonable. The budgeted dollar amounts for known agile-driven plus probable agile-driven and known plan-driven plus probable plan-driven projects were compared using a difference of means test. In terms of budgeted dollars and at the 99% confidence level, known agile-driven plus probable agile-driven projects were significantly smaller that known plan-driven plus probable plan-driven projects. This means that in terms of project size, agile-driven software development projects fit the conventional wisdom, and were significantly smaller than plan-driven software development projects. However, no similar frequency data were found for plan-driven software development projects.

Because Fleming and Koppleman (2000), Kerzner (2006), Meredith and Mantel (2003), and Schwalbe (2006) all agreed that the actual costs of software development projects were poorly managed, the actual dollars spent were estimated employing the risk factors found in Cooper et al. (2005). Furthermore, the mean number of person hours expended per project team member, the average budgeted dollars per project team member, and the estimated mean actual dollars spent per project team member were calculated. The results indicated that known agile-driven plus probable agile-driven projects were slightly more efficient in terms of the number of person hours expended, but cost substantially more in terms of the mean budgeted dollar amounts and estimated actual dollar amounts spent on a project.

When the duration of the projects were considered, the results were also quite interesting. At the 99% confidence level, known agile-driven plus probable agile-driven projects occurred significantly longer ago than plan-driven plus probable plan-driven projects. In terms of the estimated project durations, at the 99% confidence level, known agile-driven plus probable agile-driven projects were again significantly shorter than known plan-driven plus probable plan-driven projects. However, when the actual duration of the projects were considered, known agile-driven plus probable agile-driven projects were significantly shorter at the 95% confidence level than known plan-driven plus probable plan-driven projects. A short discussion ensued where the mean actual duration of the projects were compared with the average number of person hours expended. The average actual duration for a known agile-driven plus probable agile-driven project in this study was compared to the results in Cao (2006) using a difference of means test. It was found that known agile-driven plus probable agile-driven projects seemed to be growing shorter, indicating that agile-driven projects may be experiencing production efficiencies (Krugman & Wells, 2006). However, no similar frequency data were found for plan-driven software development projects.

The characters of the participants were then analyzed. By using a difference of means test, it was seen that in terms of the number of years in the selected occupation, there no statistical difference at the 95% confidence level between respondents engaged in known agile-driven plus probable agile-driven projects and respondents involved with known plan-driven plus probable probable-driven projects. At the 99% confidence level, the participants that reported on known agile-driven plus probable agile-driven projects were significantly younger than the participants that provided data on known plan-driven plus probable plan-driven projects. As for the occupational classification, the major role played in a projects, and gender, there did not seem to be any significant differences among the participants when he or she were broken into known agile-driven plus probable agile-driven projects and known plan-driven plus probable plan-driven projects.

The most significant problem encountered was analyzed. Of the responses listed in question 42, the largest response was that the project specifications were not clearly understood by the project team. The percentage that was reported was about 5% higher for known agile-driven plus probable agile-driven projects than for known plan-driven plus probable plan-driven projects.

When the software development methodology was known, the magnitude and the signs of the non-standardized estimates for the constant term and the coefficients of the dummy variable when applicable, product quality, project team effectiveness, and project management effectiveness were analyzed. Because the non-standardized estimate of the coefficient for the dummy variable was not statistically significant at the 99% confidence level, it was argued that the constant term represented the level of autonomous customer satisfaction for both agile-driven and plan-driven projects, regardless of whether the software development methodology was known, or not necessarily known. In other words, the null hypothesis H0 could not be rejected at the 99% confidence level. The magnitude and the signs for the non-standardized estimates of the coefficients for product quality and project team effectiveness were consistent with the predictions of the literature. The sign for the non-standardized estimate of the coefficient of project management effectiveness was negative, and it again argued that this result was consistent with the expectations of Christensen (1997), Desaulniers and Anderson (2001), and Kerzner (2006).

The regression findings indicated that when the software development methodology was known, the contribution to the level of autonomous customer satisfaction from known agile-driven plus probable agile-driven projects was statistically insignificant at the 95% confidence level. The reasons why the null hypothesis H0 could not be rejected were then explored. When the cost of the projects as perceived by the participants were examined, it was seen that the respondents believed that the project that he or she reported on was believed in many cases to be about the same or lower in price than other software development projects similar in size. Furthermore, when the value of the projects were studied, the participants felt that the project under consideration was usually of good to excellent value. It was then suggested that the participants could have been somewhat short sighted when he or she made the comparison with other projects. In other words, a respondent could have used as a basis of comparison projects that employed the same software development methodology as the given project.

Next, the non-standardized coefficients of the regression equation with a dummy variable and where the software development methodology was known were compared by using a difference of means test with the non-standardized coefficients of the regression equation with a dummy variable and where the software development methodology was not necessarily known. In this case, the difference of means tests showed that the constant term and the non-standardized coefficients of product quality and project management effectiveness were statistically significant at the 99% confidence level. However, the non-standardized estimates of the coefficients for the dummy variable and project team effectiveness were only statistically insignificant at the 95% confidence level. In other words, when the dummy variable was present in the regressions, the level of autonomous customer satisfaction was significantly greater when the software development methodology was known than when it was not necessarily known. The arguments provided by Brace and Brace-Pellillo (2009) and Bonferroni (1935, 1936) were outlined in detail, stating that because the customer satisfaction, product quality, project team effectiveness, and project management effectiveness variable all contained averaged data, the 99% confidence level was the more appropriate significance level to employ. Furthermore, if the Brace and Brace-Pellillo (2009) and Bonferroni (1935, 1936) suggestions are rejected, then two additional arguments were presented to show that the 99% confidence level was indeed the appropriate level of significance to use. The reasons why the null hypothesis H0 cannot be rejected were reviewed for a second time, and it was shown that the previously stated reasons remained valid.

Finally, for the regression analysis, the non-standardized coefficients of the regression equation without a dummy variable and where the software development methodology was known were compared by using a difference of means test with the non-standardized coefficients of the regression equation without a dummy variable and where the software development methodology was not necessarily known. In this case, the difference of means tests showed that the constant term and the non-standardized coefficients of product quality and project management effectiveness were statistically significant at the 99% confidence level. However, the non-standardized estimate of the coefficient for project team effectiveness was statistically significant at the 95% confidence level, but not at the 99% confidence level. In other words, when there it was assumed that there was no statistically significant difference in autonomous customer satisfaction based on the software development methodology used, at the 99% confidence level there remained a statistically significant difference in autonomous customer satisfaction and product quality when the software development methodology was known.

The last articles of data that were analyzed were the additional comments by the participants. The data indicated that when a comment was provided, those respondents that were engaged in known agile-driven plus probable agile-driven projects were concerned about the content of the software development project under consideration and the agile-driven methodology that was used. In contrast, for respondents that were involved in known plan-driven plus probable plan-driven software development projects, only the workings of the project reported on was the issue. This apparent difference of concerns was attributed to relative newness of agile-driven software development methodologies.

Conclusions

The conclusions from this study are simple. Essentially, it was shown that project that were reported on in this study were representative software development projects. For the agile-driven projects, this means that the criticism that could be leveled by the agile-driven community that the data were somehow skewed is probably not correct. Based on the size of the projects, it appeared that the known agile-driven plus probable agile-driven projects in this study represented typical agile-driven projects as understood by the agile-driven community (Chin, 2004; Highsmith, 2004; Schwaber, 2004). In terms of project durations, the known agile-driven plus probable agile-driven projects in this study were consistent with the results provided by a previous study (Cao, 2006). As for the characteristics of the participants, it appeared that except for approximate ages of the project team members, there were no statistically significant differences between project team members involved in known agile-driven plus probable agile-driven project and project team members engaged in known plan-driven plus probable plan driven projects. Thus, it was concluded that the 185 participants included in this study were indeed a representative sample.

From the regression equations, there was no statistically significant difference in autonomous customer satisfaction at the 95% confidence level for known agile-driven projects and known plan-driven projects. This comes from the fact that the null hypothesis H0 could cannot be rejected at the 95% confidence level when the software development methodology was known. Furthermore, for known agile-driven plus probable agile-driven projects and for known plan-driven plus probable plan-driven projects there was no statistically significant difference in autonomous customer satisfaction at the 99% confidence level, even though there was a statistically significant difference at the 95% confidence level. If the Brace and Brace-Pellillo (2009) and Bonferroni (1935, 1936) arguments are accepted, the conclusion from this study was that there was no statistically significant difference in autonomous customer satisfaction when the software development methodology was not necessarily known. Thus, no matter how the data were viewed, there was apparently no statistically significant difference in autonomous customer satisfaction between the use and results of agile-driven software development methods and the use and results of plan-driven software development methods.

The only other conclusion that could be made from the data in this study was that knowledge of the software development methodology resulted in a statistically significant difference at the 99% confidence level in autonomous customer satisfaction, and the non-standardized estimates of the coefficients for product quality and project management effectiveness. For project team effectiveness, there was a statistically insignificant difference when the software development methodology was known but not when the software development methodology was not necessarily known. When the dummy variable was removed from the regression equation, then and only then was non-standardized estimate of the coefficient of project team effectiveness statistically significant at the 95% level, but not at the 99% confidence level. By accepting the Brace and Brace-Pellillo (2009) and the Bonferroni (1935, 1936) suggestions, then there was no statistically significant difference in the non-standardized estimate of the coefficient of project team effectiveness when the software development methodology was known versus when the software development methodology was not necessarily known. In other words, in terms of the knowledge of the software development methodology, autonomous customer satisfaction, product quality, and project management effectiveness did matter, whereas project team effectiveness did not matter.

Recommendations

At the beginning of this study, a seemingly simple question was asked: Is customer satisfaction for software development projects significantly greater when using agile-driven methods or when employing plan-driven methods? The answer that was provided herein was that there was insufficient evidence gathered to reject the null hypothesis H0 that in the use and results of agile-driven software development methods, the level of customer satisfaction is the same as the use and results of plan-driven software development methods. At the 99% confidence level, it did not matter if the participants explicitly knew what software development methodology was employed. The use and results of agile-driven software development methods did not significantly contribute to an increase in autonomous customer satisfaction above and beyond autonomous customer satisfaction in the use and results of plan-driven software development methods.

An obvious recommendation is to redo this study employing different data, but use the same questionnaire contained in Appendix C. In the course of the analysis, there was the implied recommendation given to add a question to the survey, asking a respondent to estimate the actual dollars spent on the software development project under consideration. This was an important question to ask, for money really does matter when it comes to customer satisfaction. Even so, the hope of this researcher was to follow the data where ever it led, and then stop when the flow of the investigation came to an additional research question.

In the previous chapter, several questions were asked that bear being repeated. They include:

1. Why was the mean number of person hours expended in an agile-driven software development project so much lower than the number of person hours expended in a plan-driven software development project? Was this a case of a systematic underreporting of the number of person hours expended by those individuals involved in agile-driven projects?

2. When asked questions on project cost and value, what would have been the result if a participant that was involved in an agile-driven project was asked about a project similar in size, but the project employed plan-driven methods?

3. When asked questions on project cost and value, what would have been the result if a participant that was involved in a plan-driven project was asked about a project similar in size, but the project employed agile-driven methods?

4. What were the perceived average actual dollar amounts spent for agile-driven and plan-driven projects? Did these amounts differ from the monies actually spent? If so, how so and why?

5. On the average, why did agile-driven projects take just as much time in actual months as plan-driven projects, particularly when agile-driven projects as promoted by Highsmith (2004), Schwaber (2004), and others seemed to be more efficient and effective?

6. Considering Cao (2006), has Scrum become the dominant agile-driven software development methodology as defined by Utterback (1996)?

7. Were project team members becoming more familiar with agile-driven methodologies, and thus were agile-driven projects experiencing production efficiencies as defined by Krugman and Wells (2006)?

8. In the information technology labor market, was experience with agile-driven software development methods worth more in terms of dollars than experience in using plan-driven methods?

9. Because agile-methods are perceived by some individuals to be more egalitarian, why were the percentages of males and females engaged in agile-driven and plan-driven projects approximately the same?

10. Who were better acquainted with the software development methods that he or she employed, project team members that were engaged in agile-driven projects or project team members that were involved with plan-driven projects?

11. Why were participants in agile-driven projects concerned about the agile-driven methodologies and the outcome of the project, rather than just the outcome of the project?

12. Who had a better understanding of the products and services in a firm where he or she worked, individuals engaged in agile-driven projects or individuals involved with plan-driven projects?

Here are the questions that arose from this study. The hope was to examine empirically the basic principles of the *Agile Manifesto*, and to see if agile-driven methods did indeed promote customer satisfaction over and above plan-driven software development methods. The only reasonable conclusion that could be made from this study is that the jury is still out, continuing to sift through the data. Perhaps with more evidence, a verdict will be forthcoming? Time will tell.

REFERENCES

Aaen, I., Botcher, P., & Mathiassen, L. (1997). Software factories: Contributions and illusions. *Proceedings of the Twentieth Information Systems Research Seminar in Scandinavia*, Oslo, Norway.

Aczel, A. D., & Sounderpandian, J. (2002). *Complete business statistics* (5th. ed.). New York: McGraw-Hill.

Ambler, S. W. (2006). Initiating an agile project. *Dr. Dobb's Journal*, *31*(7), 66-68.

Ambler, S. W. (2005). Quality in an agile world. *Software Quality Professional*, *7*(4), 34-41.

Ambler, S. W. (2004). Managers manage. *Software Development*, *10*, 43-45.

Ambler, S. W. (2002). Know the user before implementing a system. *Computing Canada*, *28*(3), 13.

Ambler, S. W., & Jeffries, R. (2002). *Agile Modeling: Effective Practices for Extreme Programming and the Unified Process*. New York: John Wiley & Sons.

American Psychological Association. (2002). *Ethical principles for psychologists and code of conduct*. Retrieved June 22, 2006 from http://www.apa.org/ethics/code2002.html

Ananthpadmanabhan, H., Kale, C. Khambatti, M., Jin, Y., et al. (n.d.). Cleanroom software development. Arizona State University. Retrieved on July 7, 2007 from http://khambatti.com/mujtaba/ArticlesAndPapers/Cleanroom%20Software%20Develo pment.pdf

Anderson, D. J. (2004). *Agile management for software engineering: Applying the theory of constraints for business results*. Upper Saddle River, NJ: Pearson Education.

Baheti, P., Gehringer, E., & Stotts, D. (2002). Exploring the efficacy of distributed pair programming. *Extreme Programming and Agile Methods - XP/Agile Universe 2002 Second XP Universe and First Agile Universe Conference. Proceedings* (Lecture Notes in Computer Science Vol.2418). Berlin, Germany: Springer-Verlag, 208-228.

Beck, K., & Andres, C. (2004). *Extreme programming explained: Embrace change* (2nd ed.). Reading, MA: Addison-Wesley Longman.

Beck, K., Beedle, M., van Bennekum, A., Cockburn, A., Cunningham, W., Fowler, M., et al. (2001). *Manifesto for agile software development*. Retrieved April 7, 2004, from http://agilemanifesto.org/

Beck, K., & Fowler, M. (2000). *Planning extreme programming*. Reading, MA: Addison-Wesley Professional.

Bemer, R. W. (1968, October 7-11)). The economics of program production. *Proceedings of the IFIP Congress: Booklet I*, 13-14.

Boehm, B. & Turner, R. (2004). *Balancing agility and discipline: A guide for the perplexed.* Boston: Pearson Education.

Bonferroni, C. E. (1936). Teoria statistica delle classi e calcolo delle probabilità. *Pubblicazioni del R Istituto Superiore di Scienze Economiche e Commerciali di Firenze,* 8, 3-62.

Bonferroni, C. E. (1935). Il calcolo delle assicurazioni su gruppi di teste. In *Studi in Onore del Professore Salvatore Ortu Carboni.* Rome, Italy, 13-60.

Brace, C. H., & Brace-Pellillo, C. (2009). *Understandable statistics,* (9th ed.). Boston: Houghton-Mifflin.

Bureau of Labor Statistics. (2008, March) *Occupational outlook handbook,* (2008-09 ed.). Retrieved March 2, 2008 from http://www.bls.gov/oco/home.htm

Cao, D. B. (2006). An empirical investigation of critical success factors in agile software development projects. *ProQuest Information and Learning Company.* (UMI No. 3238566)

Cao, L. (2005). Modeling dynamics in agile software development. *ProQuest Information and Learning Company.* (UMI No. 3197587)

Charette, R. N. (2002). Foundations of lean development: The lean development manager's guide, Vol. 2, *The foundations series on risk management.* Spotsylvania, VA: ITABHI Corporation.

Chin, G. (2004). *Agile project management: How to succeed in the face of changing project requirements.* New York: AMACOM.

Chow, G. C. (1960). Tests of equality between sets of coefficients in two linear regressions. *Econometrica,* 28, 591-605.

Chrissis, M. B., Konrad, M., & Shrum, S. (2006). *CMMI: Guidelines for process integration and product improvement,* (2nd ed.). Reading, MA: Addison-Wesley Professional.

Christensen, C. M. (1997). *The innovator's dilemma: The revolutionary book that will change the way you do business.* New York: Harper Collins Publishers.

Churchill, G. A., & Surprenant, C. (1982). An investigation into the determinants of consumer satisfaction. *Journal of Marketing Research,* 19, 491-504.

Coad, P., Lefebvre, E. & De Luca, J. (1999). *Java modeling in color with UML: Enterprise components and process.* Upper Saddle River, NJ: Prentice-Hall.

Cockburn, A. (2004). *Crystal clear: A human-powered methodology for small teams.* Reading, MA: Addison-Wesley Professional.

Compact Oxford English Dictionary (2nd ed. revised). (2003). Oxford, England: Oxford University Press.

158

Cooper, D., Grey, S., Raymond, G., & Walker, P. (2005). *Project management risk guide: Managing risk in large projects and complex procurements.* West Sussex, England: John Wiley & Sons.

Covey, S. R. (1989). *The seven habits of highly effective people: Restoring the character ethic.* New York: Simon & Schuster.

Cozby, P. C. (2004). *Methods in behavioral research* (8th ed.). Boston: McGraw-Hill.

Cronbach, L. J. (1951). Coefficient alpha and the internal structure of tests. *Psychometrika, 16(3)*, 297-334.

Cusumano, M. F. (1989, March). The software factory: A historical interpretation. *IEEE Software Magazine*, 23-30.

Cusumano, M. F. (1988, July). The software factory: Origins and popularity in Japan. *MIT Sloan School of Management*, Working Paper 2036-88.

Deming, W. E. (1982). *Out of the Crisis.* Cambridge, MA: The MIT Press.

Desaulniers, D. H., & Anderson, R. J. (2001). Matching software development life cycles to the project environment. *Proceedings of the Project Management Institute 32nd Symposium,* 2001, Nashville, TN, CID: 591.

Dyer, M. (1992). *The cleanroom approach to quality software development.* New York: John Wiley & Sons.

Engle, J. F., & Blackwell, R. D. (1982). *Consumer behavior.* New York: Holt, Rinehart, and Winston.

Erdogmus, H. (2003). The economics of software development by pair programmers. *The Engineering Economist, 48*(4), 283-319.

Eyde, L. D. (2000). Other responsibilities to participants. In B. D. Sales & S. Folkman (Eds.), *Ethics in research with human participants* (pp. 61-73). Washington, D.C.: American Psychological Association.

Fischman, M. W. (2000). Informed consent. In B. D. Sales & S. Folkman (Eds.), *Ethics in research with human participants* (pp. 35-48). Washington, D.C.: American Psychological Association.

Fleming, Q. W., & Koppleman, J. M. (2000). *Earned value project management,* (2nd ed.). Newtown Square, PA: Project Management Institute.

Goldratt, E. (1990). *What is this thing called theory of constraints and how should it be implemented?* Great Barrington, MA: North River Press.

Gray, C. F., & Larson, E. W. (2006). *Project management: The managerial process* (3rd ed.). Boston: McGraw-Hill.

Gray, L. (1999). A comparison of IEEE/EIA 12207, ISO/IEC 12207, J-STD-016, and MIL-STD-498 for acquirers and developers. *Abelia Corporation*. Retrieved on June 26, 2007 from http://www.abelia.com/docs/122_016.pdf

Greenfield, J., Short, K., Cook, S., & Kent, S. (2004). *Software factories: Assembling applications with patterns, models, frameworks, and tools*. Indianapolis, IN: Wiley Publishing.

Hausler, P. A., Linger, R. C., & Trammell, C. J. (1994, March). Adopting cleanroom engineering with a phased approach. *IBM Systems Journal*, 33(1), 89-109.

Hayes, B. E. (1998). *Measuring customer satisfaction: Survey design, use, and statistical analysis methods* (2nd ed.). Milwaukee, WI: American Society for Quality.

Highsmith, J. (2004). *Agile project management: Creating innovative products*. Reading, MA: Addison Wesley Longman.

Highsmith, J. (2001). *History: The agile manifesto*. Retrieved on September 23, 2006 fromhttp://www.agilemanifesto.org/history.html

Highsmith, J. (2000). *Adaptive software development: A collaborative approach to managing complex systems*. New York: Dorset House.

Hooper, J. (2002). The Process Approach to Quality Management Systems. In the ASQ ISO 9000:2000 Handbook. In C. A. Cianfrani, J. J. Tsiakals, & J. E. West (Eds.). *The ASQ ISO 9000-2000 handbook*. Milwaukee, WI: ASQ Quality Press.

Howard, J., & Sheth, J. (1969). *The theory of buyer behavior*. New York: John Wiley & Sons.

Humphrey, W. S. (1999). *Introduction to the team software process*. Reading, MA: Addison-Wesley Professional.

Humphrey, W. S. (1996). *Introduction to the personal software process*. Reading, MA: Addison-Wesley Professional.

Humphrey, W. S. (1995). *A discipline for software engineering*. Reading, MA: Addison-Wesley Longman.

Humphrey, W. S. (1989). *Managing the software process*. Reading, MA: Addison-Wesley.

Humphrey, W. S. (1987, June). Characterizing the software process: A maturity framework. *Software Engineering Institute,* CMU/SEI-87-TR-11, DTIC Number ADA 182195.

Hunt, K. H. (1977). CS/D – Overview and future research direction. In K. H. Hunt (Ed.), *Conceptualization and Measurement of Consumer Satisfaction and Dissatisfaction*. Cambridge, MA: Marketing Science Institute.

Jeffries, R., Anderson, A., & Hendrickson, C. (2000). *Extreme programming installed*. Reading, MA: Addison-Wesley Professional.

Kan, S. H. (1995). *Metrics and models in software quality engineering.* Reading, MA: Addison Wesley Longman.

Kerzner, H. (2006). *Project management: A systems approach to planning, scheduling and controlling* (9th ed.). New York: John Wiley & Sons.

Koutsoyiannis, A. (1977). *Theory of econometrics: An introductory exposition of econometric methods,* (2nd ed.). London: The Macmillan Press.

Kouzes, J. M., & Pozner, B. Z. (1987). *The leadership challenge: How to get extraordinary things done in organizations.* San Francisco, CA: Jossey-Bass Publishers.

Krugman, P. & Wells, R. (2006). *Economics.* New York: Worth Publishers.

Kulpa, M. K. (2003). *Interpreting the CMMI: A process improvement approach.* Boca Raton, FL: Auerbach Publications.

Kutner, M. H., Nachtsheim, C. J., Neter, J., & Li, W. (2004). *Applied linear statistical models.* New York: McGraw-Hill/Irwin.

Linger, R. C., & Trammell, C. J. (1996). *Cleanroom software engineering implementation of the CMM for software* (CMU/SEI-96-TR-23). Pittsburgh, PA: Carnegie-Mellon University, Software Engineering Institute.

MacMillan, J., & Vosburgh, J. R. (1986). *Software quality indicators.* Cambridge, MA: Scientific Systems.

McCall, J. A. (1979). *An introduction to software quality metrics.* In J. D. Cooper & M. J. Fisher (Eds.), Software Quality Management. New York: A Petrocelli Book.

McIlroy, M. D. (1968, October 7-11). Mass produced software components. *Report NATO Conference on Software Engineering,* Garmish, 138-152.

Meredith, J. R., & Mantel, S. J. Jr. (2003). *Project management: A managerial approach* (5th ed.). New York: John Wiley & Sons.

Mills, H. D., Dyer, M., & Linger, R. C. (1987, September). Cleanroom software engineering. *IEEE Software,* pp. 19-24.

Murine, G. E. (1988). Integrating software quality metrics with software QA. *Quality Progress, 21*(11), 38-43.

National Institutes of Health. (2005, June 23). Regulations and ethical guidelines, Title 45: Public Welfare, Part 46: Protection of Human Subjects. Retrieved June 23, 2006 from http://ohsr.od.nih.gov/guidelines/45cfr46.html

Nawrocki, J. R., Jasinski, M., Walter, B., & Wojceichowski, A. (2002). Extreme programming modified: Embrace requirements engineering practices. *Proceedings of the IEEE Joint International Conference on Requirements Engineering,* 3.

Paulk, M. C., Curtis, B., & Chrissis, M. B. (1991, August). Capability maturity model for software. *Software Engineering Institute*, CMU/SEI-91-TR-24, DTIC Number ADA263403.

Paulk, M. C., Weber, C. V., Curtis, B., & Chrissis, M. B. (Eds.). (1994). *The capability maturity model: Guidelines for improving the software process.* Boston: Addison-Wesley Longman.

Peach, R. W. (Ed.). (1997). *The ISO 9000 handbook*, (3rd ed.). New York: McGraw-Hill.

Piore, M. J., & Sabel, C. F. (1984). *The second industrial divide: Possibilities for prosperity.* New York: Basic Books.

Poppendieck, M., & Poppendieck, T. (2006). *Lean software development: An agile toolkit for software managers.* Reading, MA: Addison-Wesley.

Project Management Institute. (2005). *A guide to the project management body of knowledge: PMBOK guide 2005 edition.* Newton Square, PA: Project Management Institute.

Prowell, S. J., Trammell, C. J., Linger, R. C., & Poore, J. H. (1999). *Cleanroom software engineering: Technology and process.* Boston: Addison-Wesley Professional.

Rising, L., & Derby, E. (2003). Singing the songs of project experience: patterns and retrospectives. *Cutter IT Journal, 16*(9), 27-33.

Sales, B. D., & Lavin, M. (2000). Identifying conflicts of interest and resolving ethical dilemmas. In B. D. Sales & S. Folkman (Eds.), *Ethics in research with human participants* (pp. 109-128). Washington, D.C.: American Psychological Association.

Satterthwaite, F. E. (1946). An approximate distribution of estimates of variance components. *Biometrics Bulletin 2*, 110-114.

Scholtes, P. R. (1988). *The team handbook: How to use teams to improve quality.* Madison, WI: Joiner Associates Consulting Group.

Schulmeyer, G. G. (1999). Software quality assurance metrics. In G. G. Schulmeyer & J. I. McManus (Eds.), *Handbook of software quality assurance*, (3rd ed.). Upper Saddle River, NJ: Prentice-Hall.

Schwaber, K. (2004). *Agile project management with Scrum.* Upper Saddle River, NJ: Prentice-Hall.

Schwaber, K. (1996, April). Controlled chaos: Living on the edge. *American Programmer, 5,* 10-16.

Schwalbe, K. (2006). *Information technology: Project management,* (4th ed.). Boston: Thompson Course Technology.

Scott-Jones, D. (2000). Recruitment of research participants. In B. D. Sales & S. Folkman (Eds.), *Ethics in research with human participants* (pp. 27-34). Washington, D.C.: American Psychological Association.

162

Senge, P. M., Kleiner, A., Roberts, C., Ross, R., & Smith, B. (1994). *The fifth discipline fieldbook.* New York: Doubleday Press.

Sieber, J. E. (1992). *Planning ethically responsible research: A guide for students and internal review boards.* Newbury Park, CA: Sage Publications.

Sieber, J. E. (2000). Planning research: Basic ethical decision making. In B. D. Sales & S. Folkman (Eds.), *Ethics in research with human participants* (pp. 13-26). Washington, D.C.: American Psychological Association.

Smith, M. B. (2000). Moral foundations of research with human participants. In B. D. Sales & S. Folkman (Eds.), *Ethics in research with human participants* (pp. 3-10). Washington, D.C.: American Psychological Association.

Spunt, T. M. (1999). *Guide to customer surveys: Sample questionnaires and detailed guidelines for creating effective surveys.* New York: The Customer Service Group.

Solomon, P. (2002, October). Using CMMI to improve earned value management. *CMU/SEI-2002-TN-016.* Software Engineering Institute. Retrieved on July 16, 2007 from http://www.sei.cmu.edu/pub/documents/02.reports/pdf/02tn016.pdf

SurveyGold survey software. (2008). [Computer software and manual]. *Golden Hills Software, Inc.* Retrieved March 1, 2008, from http://surveygold.com/download.htm

Takeuchi, H., & Nonaka, I. (1986, January-February). The new new product development game. *Harvard Business School Review.*

Taylor, F. W. (1911). *The principles of scientific management.* New York: Harper & Brothers.

Trochim, W. K. (2001). *The Research methods knowledge base* (2nd. ed.). Cincinnati, OH: Atomic Dog Publishing.

Tse, D. K., & Wilton, P. C. (1988). Models of consumer satisfaction: An extension. *Journal of Marketing Research, 25*(2), 204-212.

Turner, R., & Jain, A. (2002). Agile meets CMMI: Culture clash or common cause?. *Extreme Programming and Agile Methods – X/P Agile Universe 2002,* 153-165.

Utterback, J. (1996). *Mastering the dynamics of innovation: How companies can seize opportunity in the face of technological change.* Boston: Harvard Business School Press.

Varva, T. G. (1997). *Improving your measurement of customer satisfaction: A guide to creating, conducting, analyzing, and reporting customer satisfaction measurement programs.* Milwaukee, WI: American Society for Quality.

Weber, C. V., Paulk, M. C., Wise, C. J., & Withey, J. (1991, August). *Key practices of the capability maturity model.* Software Engineering Institute, CMU/SEI-91-Tr-25 DTIC Number ADA 240604.

Web Studio 4.0 software. (2008). [Computer software and manual]. *Back to the Beach Software, LLC.* Retrieved January 2, 2008, from https://www.webstudio.com/site/DownloadRegistration.asp

Welch, B. L. (1947). The generalization of "student's" problem when several different population variances are involved. *Biometrika* 34, 28-35.

Westbrook, R. A., & Reilly, M. D. (1983). Value – percept disparity: An alternative to the disconfirmation of expectations theory of consumer satisfaction. In R. P. Bagozzi & A. M. Tybout (Eds.), *Advances in Consumer Research*. Ann Arbor, MI: Association for Consumer Research.

APPENDIX A – CONSENT FORM

600 N. Plankinton Ave.
Milwaukee, WI 53201-3005
t: 414-272-8575
800 248 1946
f 414-272-1734
www.asq.org

AMERICAN SOCIETY
FOR QUALITY

October 5, 2007

Donald L. Buresh
3115 Enoch Avenue
Zion, IL 60099
Phone: (847) 872-1659

Dear Don:

We are pleased to grant you non-exclusive world rights to reproduce the following material:

Item: Figure 2.3, page 15
From: *Measuring Customer Satisfaction, Second Edition*
By: Bob E. Hayes
ISBN: 0-87389-362-X
Copyright Yr: 1998

This material is to be used in a dissertation on customer satisfaction and agile project management. Copyright clearance is granted for this use.

The following acknowledgement must appear below the table:

Portions reproduced by permission of Bob E. Hayes, *Measuring Customer Satisfaction: Survey Design, Use, and Statistical Analysis Methods, Second Edition* (Milwaukee: ASQ Quality Press, 1998). To order this book, call ASQ at 800-248-1946 or 414-272-8575, or visit http://www.asq.org/quality-press.

There is no fee for this use.

This permission is valid only for the use specifically described in this agreement. Any other use requires separate permission. Please contact me if you have any questions.

Sincerely,

Paul O'Mara, CQIA
Project Editor
ASQ Quality Press

APPENDIX B – EMAIL LETTER TO POTENTIAL PARTICIPANTS

Please distribute this email. Data on both agile and plan-driven projects are welcome.

To Whom It May Concern,

My name is Donald Buresh, and I am a Ph.D. student at Northcentral University located in Prescott Valley, Arizona. The reason that I am writing to you is because I would like you to participate in an internet survey for my dissertation. The topic of my dissertation is assessing agile project management and customer satisfaction. The web site where you can find my survey is: www.assessingagilepm.com.

The questionnaire will ask you about a software development project that was recently completed within your organization. It will take you about 15 minutes to answer the questions. The questionnaire will ask you a series of questions about the project, including whether the software product was developed using agile-driven or plan-driven methods. If you do not know the answer, the questionnaire will ask you a series of three questions, and based on your responses, it is smart enough to decide what software methodology was employed. The questionnaire will then ask you other questions about the software development project. If at any time you decide not to participate in the survey, you need only exit the survey window, and your data will not be collected. When you have completed the survey, please press the appropriate button to submit your responses, and then close the survey window.

All of your responses will be anonymous and all of your data will be held in the strictest confidence. From your responses, it will not be possible to identify you or your organization. Since the data obtained from this questionnaire will be used in my doctoral dissertation, the results may possibly appear in an academic or trade publication. None of your responses will ever be revealed.

Thank you for considering to participate in this survey. If you do participate in the survey, and want to obtain a copy of my dissertation, please do not hesitate to respond to this email, and let me know. When the degree has been granted, and the dissertation has been accepted and published, I will be more than happy to send you an electronic copy. Again, thank you for your time.

Donald L. Buresh
3115 Enoch Avenue
Zion, IL 60099
Home Tele: 847-872-1659

APPENDIX C – QUESTIONNAIRE

Assessing Customer Satisfaction and Agile Methods

Questionnaire Instructions

The purpose of this questionnaire is to collect customer satisfaction data regarding the results from using a specific agile or plan-driven software development methodology. There are 51 questions contained in this questionnaire. All responses will be anonymous and all data will be held in the strictest confidence. From your responses, it will not be possible to identify specific individuals or companies. The data obtained from this questionnaire will be used in a doctoral dissertation. The results may possibly appear in an academic or trade publication. No individual responses will be revealed. By pressing the **Continue** button you are initially agreeing to participate in the study. To include your data in the study you must press the **Submit Your Responses** button that appears at the end of the questionnaire. At any point in time, if you close this window, any data that you previously provided will **not** be included in the study.

Please press the Continue *button if you choose initially to participate in the study.*

Please close this window if you do not want to participate in the study.

Project Information Instructions - Project Name

The following nine questions are concerned with the overall characteristics of your project. The topics include the name of the project, the software methodology used, the number of person hours expended, the number of individuals on the project team, the size of the budget, how long ago was the project completed, and the estimated and actual duration of the project. Please respond to all of the questions in this section of the questionnaire.

Percent Completed: **0.0%**

Please press the Go Back *button if you want to review and/or change your response to the previous question.*

Please press the Continue *button when you are satisfied with your response*

1. Please enter the name of the project.
   (Provide one response only.)

Project Information - Methodology Used

Percent Completed: **2.0%**

Please press the Go Back *button if you want to review and/or change your response to the previous question.*

Please press the Continue *button when you are satisfied with your response.*

2. What type of software development method was used in this project?
(Select only one.)
☐ Agile software development methods.
☐ Plan-driven software development methods.
☐ Do not know what type of software development methodology was used.

Project Information - Agile Methodologies

Percent Completed: **3.9%**

Please press the Go Back *button if you want to review and/or change your response to the previous question.*

Please press the Continue *button when you are satisfied with your response.*

3. What type of agile software development methodology was used?
(Select only one.)
☐ Extreme Programming
☐ Adaptive Software Development
☐ Crystal Methods
☐ Scrum
☐ Feature Driven Development
☐ Dynamic Systems Development
☐ Lean Development
☐ Other method:
☐ Do not know what type of agile software development methodology was used.

Project Information - Plan-Driven Methodologies

Percent Completed: **3.9%**

Please press the Go Back *button if you want to review and/or change your response to the previous question.*

Please press the Continue *button when you are satisfied with your response.*

3. What type of plan-driven software development methodology was used?
(Select only one.)
☐ Military Standards
☐ ISO Standard
☐ EIA Standard
☐ IEEE Standard
☐ Software Factory
☐ Cleanroom Methodology
☐ Capability Maturity Model
☐ Capability Maturity Model Integration
☐ Personal Software Process
☐ Team Software Process
☐ Other method:
☐ Do not know what type of plan-driven software development methodology was used.

The following three questions are concerned with characterizing the type of software development methodology used in your project. The topics include questions on the project plan, the project environment, and the project management. Please respond to all of the questions in this section of the questionnaire.

Percent Completed: **3.9%**

Please press the Go Back *button if you want to review and/or change your response to the previous question.*

Please press the Continue *button when you are satisfied with your response.*

3a. The project plan can be characterized by:
(Select only one.)
- ☐   Rapid value and responsiveness to change as a means to an end.
- ☐   Predictability, stability, and high assurance to anchor project processes.

Percent Completed: **4.6%**

Please press the Go Back *button if you want to review and/or change your response to the previous question.*

Please press the Continue *button when you are satisfied with your response.*

3b. The environment of the project can be characterized by:
(Select only one.)
- ☐   A turbulent high-change environment with some risks.
- ☐   Requirements that were largely determined in advance and remained relatively stable.

Percent Completed: **5.3%**

Please press the Go Back *button if you want to review and/or change your response to the previous question.*

Please press the Continue *button when you are satisfied with your response.*

3c. The management of the project can be characterized by:
(Select only one.)
- ☐   A dependence on dedicated customer representatives working side by side with the project team.
- ☐   A dependence on some form of contract between the project team and the customers.

Percent Completed: **5.9%**

Please press the Go Back *button if you want to review and/or change your response to the previous question.*

Please press the Continue *button when you are satisfied with your response.*

4. What was the number of person hours expended by the project?
(Select only one.)
☐   Under 1,000 person hours
☐   1,000 - 1,999
☐   2,000 - 3,999
☐   4,000 - 7,999
☐   8,000 - 11,999
☐   12,000 - 19,999
☐   20,000 or over person hours

Project Information - Number of Individuals

Percent Completed: **7.8%**

Please press the Go Back *button if you want to review and/or change your response to the previous question.*

Please press the Continue *button when you are satisfied with your response.*

5. What best describes the number of individuals on the project team?
(Select only one.)
☐   Under 10 people
☐   10 - 19 people
☐   20 - 39 people
☐   40 - 59 people
☐   60 - 79 people
☐   80 - 99 people
☐   100 people or over

Project Information - Size of the Budget

Percent Completed: **9.8%**

Please press the Go Back *button if you want to review and/or change your response to the previous question.*

Please press the Continue *button when you are satisfied with your response.*

6. What best describes the budget for this project?
(Select only one.)
☐   Under $50,000
☐   50,000 - 99,999
☐   100,000 - 249,999
☐   250,000 - 499,999

☐   500,000 - 999,999
☐   1,000,000 - 4,999,999
☐ $5,000,000 or over

Project Information - Project Completion

Percent Completed: **11.8%**

Please press the Go Back *button if you want to review and/or change your response to the previous question.*

Please press the Continue *button when you are satisfied with your response.*

7. How long ago was the project completed in actual months?
(Select only one.)
☐   Less than 1 month ago
☐   1 - 3
☐   4 - 6
☐   7 - 9
☐   10 - 12
☐   13 - 18
☐   Over 18 months ago

Project Information - Estimated Duration

Percent Completed: **13.7%**

Please press the Go Back *button if you want to review and/or change your response to the previous question.*

Please press the Continue *button when you are satisfied with your response.*

8. What was the _estimated_ duration of the project in actual months?
(Select only one.)
☐   Under 3 months
☐   4 - 6
☐   7 - 9
☐   10 - 12
☐   13 - 18
☐   19 - 24
☐   Over 24 months

Project Information - Actual Duration

Percent Completed: **15.7%**

Please press the Go Back *button if you want to review and/or change your response to the previous question.*

Please press the Continue *button when you are satisfied with your response.*

9. What was the _actual_ duration of the project in actual months?
(Select only one.)
- ☐   Under 3 months
- ☐   4 - 6
- ☐   7 - 9
- ☐   10 - 12
- ☐   13 - 18
- ☐   19 - 24
- ☐   Over 24 months

Overall Customer Satisfaction Instructions - Overall Satisfaction

The following nine questions deal with your overall customer satisfaction with the results of using the specified software development methodology in your project. The questions ask about your overall satisfaction with the results of the project, whether you would use or recommend the software development methodology employed again, the overall and relative product quality, the cost and timeliness of the project, and the value of using the selected software development methodology. Please respond to all of the questions in this section of the questionnaire.

Percent Completed: **17.6%**

Please press the Go Back *button if you want to review and/or change your response to the previous question.*

Please press the Continue *button when you are satisfied with your response.*

10. How satisfied are you overall with the results from the project?
(Select only one.)
- ☐   Extremely Dissatisfied
- ☐   Dissatisfied
- ☐   Neutral
- ☐   Satisfied
- ☐   Extremely Satisfied

Overall Customer Satisfaction - Use Software Development Methods Again

Percent Completed: **19.6%**

Please press the Go Back *button if you want to review and/or change your response to the previous question.*

Please press the Continue *button when you are satisfied with your response.*

11. How likely will it be to use the software development methods employed in this project in your next project?
(Select only one.)
- ☐   Definitely would not
- ☐   Probably would not
- ☐   Neutral
- ☐   Probably would
- ☐   Definitely would

Overall Customer Satisfaction - Use Previous Software Development Methods

Percent Completed: **21.6%**

Please press the Go Back *button if you want to review and/or change your response to the previous question.*

Please press the Continue *button when you are satisfied with your response.*

12. How likely was it to use in this project the software development methods previously employed in other projects?

(Select only one.)
- ☐   Definitely would not
- ☐   Probably would not
- ☐   Neutral
- ☐   Probably would
- ☐   Definitely would

Overall Customer Satisfaction - Recommend Software Development Methods

Percent Completed: **23.5%**

Please press the Go Back *button if you want to review and/or change your response to the previous question.*

Please press the Continue *button when you are satisfied with your response.*

13. How likely will you be to recommend to a friend or a business associate the software development methods that were used in this project?

(Select only one.)
- ☐   Definitely will not
- ☐   Probably will not
- ☐   Neutral
- ☐   Probably will
- ☐   Definitely will

Overall Customer Satisfaction - Overall Product Quality

Percent Completed: **25.5%**

Please press the Go Back *button if you want to review and/or change your response to the previous question.*

Please press the Continue *button when you are satisfied with your response.*

14. How would you rate the overall quality of the software product that was developed by this project?

(Select only one.)
- ☐   Poor
- ☐   Fair
- ☐   Good

☐   Very Good
☐   Excellent

Overall Customer Satisfaction - Relative Product Quality

Percent Completed: **27.5%**

Please press the Go Back *button if you want to review and/or change your response to the previous question.*

Please press the Continue *button when you are satisfied with your response.*

15. How would you rate the overall quality of other software products that were developed by other projects?
    (Select only one.)
☐   Poor
☐   Fair
☐   Good
☐   Very Good
☐   Excellent

Overall Customer Satisfaction - Relative Project Costs

Percent Completed: **29.4%**

Please press the Go Back *button if you want to review and/or change your response to the previous question.*

Please press the Continue *button when you are satisfied with your response.*

16. How would you compare the cost of this project with the cost of other projects similar in size?
    (Select only one.)
☐   Very low priced
☐   Low priced
☐   About the same
☐   High priced
☐   Very high priced

Overall Customer Satisfaction - Relative Project Timeliness

Percent Completed: **31.4%**

Please press the Go Back *button if you want to review and/or change your response to the previous question.*

Please press the Continue *button when you are satisfied with your response.*

17. How would you compare the ability of this project to meet its schedule with other projects similar in size?
    (Select only one.)

☐   Significantly under schedule
☐   A little under schedule
☐   Approximately on schedule
☐   A little over schedule
☐   Significantly over schedule

Overall Customer Satisfaction - All Things Considered

Percent Completed: **33.3%**

Please press the Go Back *button if you want to review and/or change your response to the previous question.*

Please press the Continue *button when you are satisfied with your response.*

18. How would you describe this project all things considered?
(Select only one.)
☐   Poor value for the money
☐   Fair value
☐   Good value
☐   Very good value
☐   Excellent value for the money

Product Quality Instructions - Meeting Specifications

This section of the questionnaire is concerned with the quality of the software product. It contains seven questions. The topics deal with meeting the software product specifications, the software product performing its intended functions, understanding how the final product works, the finding and correcting of errors during and after the software development phase, whether the product performs its intended functions, and whether the components of the product work together correctly. Please respond to all of the questions in the questionnaire.

Percent Completed: **35.3%**

Please press the Go Back *button if you want to review and/or change your response to the previous question.*

Please press the Continue *button when you are satisfied with your response.*

19. What was the degree to which the product met your specifications?
(Select only one.)
☐   Definitely did not
☐   Probably did not
☐   Neutral
☐   Probably did
☐   Definitely did

Product Quality - Performing Intended Functions

Percent Completed: **37.3%**

Please press the Go Back *button if you want to review and/or change your response to the previous question.*

Please press the Continue *button when you are satisfied with your response.*

20. How would you rate the final product in performing its intended functions?
(Select only one.)
- ☐ Poor
- ☐ Fair
- ☐ Good
- ☐ Very Good
- ☐ Excellent

Product Quality - Understanding the Final Product

Percent Completed: **39.2%**

Please press the Go Back *button if you want to review and/or change your response to the previous question.*

Please press the Continue *button when you are satisfied with your response.*

21. How much effort is required to understand how the final product works?
(Select only one.)
- ☐ Very high amount of effort
- ☐ High effort
- ☐ Average amount
- ☐ Low amount
- ☐ Very low amount of effort

Product Quality - Finding and Correcting Errors While in Development

Percent Completed: **41.2%**

Please press the Go Back *button if you want to review and/or change your response to the previous question.*

Please press the Continue *button when you are satisfied with your response.*

22. How much effort was required to find and correct errors in the product when it was in development?

(Select only one.)
- ☐ Very high amount of effort
- ☐ High amount
- ☐ Average amount
- ☐ Low amount
- ☐ Very low amount of effort

Product Quality - Finding and Correcting Errors After Development Is Completed

Percent Completed: **43.1%**

Please press the Go Back *button if you want to review and/or change your response to the previous question.*

Please press the Continue *button when you are satisfied with your response.*

23. How much effort was required to find and correct errors in the product after it was developed?

(Select only one.)

☐   Very high amount of effort
☐   High amount
☐   Average amount
☐   Low amount
☐   Very low amount of effort

Product Quality - Product Performed Intended Functions

Percent Completed: **45.1%**

Please press the Go Back *button if you want to review and/or change your response to the previous question.*

Please press the Continue *button when you are satisfied with your response.*

24. How much effort was required to ensure that the product performed its intended functions?

(Select only one.)

☐   Very high amount of effort
☐   High amount
☐   Average amount
☐   Low amount
☐   Very low amount of effort

Product Quality - Components Worked Together

Percent Completed: **47.1%**

Please press the Go Back *button if you want to review and/or change your response to the previous question.*

Please press the Continue *button when you are satisfied with your response.*

25. How much effort was required to ensure that the components within the product worked together effectively?

(Select only one.)

☐   Very high amount of effort
☐   High amount
☐   Average amount
☐   Low amount
☐   Very low amount of effort

Project Team Effectiveness Instructions - Contribution Was Appreciated

The following twelve questions address the effectiveness of the project team. The topics are concerned with whether your contribution was appreciated, whether you trusted the project team, the responsiveness of the team members, the focus and behavior of the project team, and enthusiasm of the project team. Please respond to all of the questions in this section of the questionnaire.

Percent Completed: 49.0%

Please press the Go Back *button if you want to review and/or change your response to the previous question.*

Please press the Continue *button when you are satisfied with your response.*

26. The project team made you feel that your contribution to the project was appreciated.
   (Select only one.)
   ☐   Strongly disagree
   ☐   Disagree
   ☐   Neutral
   ☐   Agree
   ☐   Strongly agree

Project Team Effectiveness - Trusted the Project Team

Percent Completed: **51.0%**

Please press the Go Back *button if you want to review and/or change your response to the previous question.*

Please press the Continue *button when you are satisfied with your response.*

27. What was your level of trust of the project team?
   (Select only one.)
   ☐   Very low level of trust
   ☐   Low level of trust
   ☐   Neutral
   ☐   High level of trust
   ☐   Very high level of trust

Project Team Effectiveness - Authority to Resolve Problems

Percent Completed: **52.9%**

Please press the Go Back *button if you want to review and/or change your response to the previous question.*

Please press the Continue *button when you are satisfied with your response.*

28. The project team had the authority to resolve problems.
   (Select only one.)
   ☐   Strongly disagree
   ☐   Disagree
   ☐   Neutral

☐ Agree
☐ Strongly agree

Project Team Effectiveness - Straightforward Answers Provided

Percent Completed: **54.9%**

Please press the Go Back *button if you want to review and/or change your response to the previous question.*

Please press the Continue *button when you are satisfied with your response.*

29. The project team provided you with straightforward answers to your questions. (Select only one.)
☐ Strongly disagree
☐ Disagree
☐ Neutral
☐ Agree
☐ Strongly agree

Project Team Effectiveness - Responsive to Issues Raised

Percent Completed: **56.9%**

Please press the Go Back *button if you want to review and/or change your response to the previous question.*

Please press the Continue *button when you are satisfied with your response.*

30. The project team was responsive to the issues that were raised during the course of the project.
(Select only one.)
☐ Strongly disagree
☐ Disagree
☐ Neutral
☐ Agree
☐ Strongly agree

Project Team Effectiveness - Issue Resolution Speed

Percent Completed: **58.8%**

Please press the Go Back *button if you want to review and/or change your response to the previous question.*

Please press the Continue *button when you are satisfied with your response.*

31. How would you rate the speed in which the project team resolved issues that were raised regarding the product?
(Select only one.)
☐ Very slow
☐ Slow

☐ Average
☐ Fast
☐ Very fast

Project Team Effectiveness - Focused on Customer Requirements and Issues

Percent Completed: **60.8%**

Please press the Go Back *button if you want to review and/or change your response to the previous question.*

Please press the Continue *button when you are satisfied with your response.*

32. *The project team was available to focus on customer requirements and issues.*
(Select only one.)
☐ Strongly disagree
☐ Disagree
☐ Neutral
☐ Agree
☐ Strongly agree

Project Team Effectiveness - Achieved Short-Term Objectives

Percent Completed: **62.7%**

Please press the Go Back *button if you want to review and/or change your response to the previous question.*

Please press the Continue *button when you are satisfied with your response.*

33. *The project team helped you achieve your short-term objectives.*
(Select only one.)
☐ Strongly disagree
☐ Disagree
☐ Neutral
☐ Agree
☐ Strongly agree

Project Team Effectiveness - Achieved Long-Term Goals

Percent Completed: **64.7%**

Please press the Go Back *button if you want to review and/or change your response to the previous question.*

Please press the Continue *button when you are satisfied with your response.*

34. *The project team helped you achieve your long-term goals.*
(Select only one.)
☐ Strongly disagree
☐ Disagree
☐ Neutral

☐   Agree
☐   Strongly agree

Project Team Effectiveness - Behaved in a Professional Manner

Percent Completed: **66.7%**

Please press the Go Back *button if you want to review and/or change your response to the previous question.*

Please press the Continue *button when you are satisfied with your response.*

35. The project team behaved in a professional manner.
(Select only one.)
☐   Strongly disagree
☐   Disagree
☐   Neutral
☐   Agree
☐   Strongly agree

Project Team Effectiveness - Enthusiastic About the Project

Percent Completed: **68.6%**

Please press the Go Back *button if you want to review and/or change your response to the previous question.*

Please press the Continue *button when you are satisfied with your response.*

36. The project team was enthusiastic about the project during the course of this project.
(Select only one.)
☐   Strongly disagree
☐   Disagree
☐   Neutral
☐   Agree
☐   Strongly agree

Project Team Effectiveness - Enthusiastic About Project Methods

Percent Completed: **70.6%**

Please press the Go Back *button if you want to review and/or change your response to the previous question.*

Please press the Continue *button when you are satisfied with your response.*

37. The project team was enthusiastic about the software development methods used during the course of this project.
(Select only one.)
☐   Strongly disagree
☐   Disagree
☐   Neutral

☐   Agree
☐   Strongly agree

Project Management Effectiveness Instructions - Timely Completion

The following four questions deal with the effectiveness of the managing the specified project using the selected software development methodology. The topics deal with the timely completion of the project, whether the software development methodology was responsible for the project's timely completion, if the project's time constraints were understood by the project manager, and if the project was completed under, on, or over budget. Please respond to all of the questions in this section of the questionnaire.

Percent Completed: **72.5%**

Please press the Go Back *button if you want to review and/or change your response to the previous question.*

Please press the Continue *button when you are satisfied with your response.*

38. Did the project finished before, approximately on, or after the scheduled completion date?
(Select only one.)
☐   Significantly ahead of schedule
☐   Ahead of schedule
☐   Approximately on schedule
☐   Behind schedule
☐   Significantly behind schedule

Project Management Effectiveness - Method Responsible for Timely Completion

Percent Completed: **74.5%**

Please press the Go Back *button if you want to review and/or change your response to the previous question.*

Please press the Continue *button when you are satisfied with your response.*

39. The software development methods used in this project were chiefly responsible for the project finishing in a timely manner.
(Select only one.)
☐   Strongly disagree
☐   Disagree
☐   Neutral
☐   Agree
☐   Strongly agree

Project Management Effectiveness - Project Manager Understood Time Constraints

Percent Completed: **76.5%**

Please press the Go Back *button if you want to review and/or change your response to the previous question.*

Please press the Continue *button when you are satisfied with your response.*

40. The project manager understood how much time the project required.
(Select only one.)
- ☐ Strongly disagree
- ☐ Disagree
- ☐ Neutral
- ☐ Agree
- ☐ Strongly agree

Project Management Effectiveness - Project Completed Under, On, or Over Budget

Percent Completed: **78.4%**

Please press the Go Back *button if you want to review and/or change your response to the previous question.*

Please press the Continue *button when you are satisfied with your response.*

41. Was the project completed under, on, or over budget?
(Select only one.)
- ☐ Significantly under budget
- ☐ Under budget
- ☐ Approximately on budget
- ☐ Over budget
- ☐ Significantly over budget

Potential Problems with the Project Instructions - Most Significant Problem Encountered

The following four questions are concerned the potential problems encountered during the course of the project. The topics include what was the most significant problem encountered during the course of the project, whether you informed the project manager or some other individual about this problem, and were you satisfied with the response from the project team. Please respond to all of the questions in this section of the questionnaire.

Percent Completed: **80.4%**

Please press the Go Back *button if you want to review and/or change your response to the previous question.*

Please press the Continue *button when you are satisfied with your response.*

42. Please select the most significant problem that was encountered during the course of the project. If you select option Q, the questionnaire will skip to question 46; otherwise the questionnaire will proceed to question 43.
(Select only one.)
- ☐ A. The project team lacked knowledge about your company's products and services.
- ☐ B. The project team was unable to recommend the best way to meet your needs.
- ☐ C. The project team did not do what you asked.
- ☐ D. The project team was not responsive to your requests.

☐   E. The project team did not do what they said that they would do.
☐   F. The project team did not return your telephone calls.
☐   G. The project team did not reply to your emails.
☐   H. The project manager was not available when you needed to see him or her.
☐   I. The attitude of the project team was not positive.
☐   J. The project team was rude, unfriendly, or inconsiderate.
☐   K. The project was not completed in a timely manner.
☐   L. The project specifications were not clearly understood.
☐   M. When a choice needed to be made, the project team did not provide a reasonable explanation.
☐   N. The project team did not contact me promptly when a mistake occurred.
☐   O. The project team did not quickly correct mistakes.
☐   P. Other:
☐   Q. No serious problems occurred in my day-to-day dealings with the project team.

Potential Problems with the Project - Informed Project Manager

Percent Completed: **82.4%**

Please press the Go Back *button if you want to review and/or change your response to the previous question.*

Please press the Continue *button when you are satisfied with your response.*

43. Did you tell the project manager about the problem?
(Select only one.)
☐   Yes
☐   No

Potential Problems with the Project - Informed Anyone Else

Percent Completed: **84.3%**

Please press the Go Back *button if you want to review and/or change your response to the previous question.*

Please press the Continue *button when you are satisfied with your response.*

44. Did you tell anyone other than the project manager about the problem?
(Select only one.)
☐   Yes
☐   No

Potential Problems with the Project - Satisfied with the Response from the Project Manager

Percent Completed: **86.3%**

Please press the Go Back *button if you want to review and/or change your response to the previous question.*

Please press the Continue *button when you are satisfied with your response.*

**45. *How satisfied were you overall response to this problem by the project manager?*
(Select only one.)**

- ☐   Not at all satisfied because no action was taken
- ☐   Not at all satisfied with the action taken
- ☐   Not completely satisfied, but some action was taken
- ☐   Not completely satisfied, but the action taken was acceptable
- ☐   Completely satisfied with the action taken

Demographic Information Instructions - Your Occupation

The following six questions inquire about your demographic data. The topics include data on your occupation, the number of years that you have been in your current occupation, you age group, your gender, and any additional concerns that you might wish to share. Please respond to all of the questions in this section of the questionnaire.

Percent Completed: **88.2%**

Please press the Go Back *button if you want to review and/or change your response to the previous question.*

Please press the Continue *button when you are satisfied with your response.*

**46. *Please select the occupational classification that is closest to your given occupation.*
(Select only one.)**

- ☐   Air transportation occupations
- ☐   Architects, surveyors, and cartographers
- ☐   Armed services occupations
- ☐   Art and design occupations
- ☐   Assemblers and fabricators
- ☐   Building and grounds cleaning and maintenance occupations
- ☐   Business and financial operations occupations
- ☐   Community and social services
- ☐   Computer and mathematical occupations
- ☐   Construction, trades and related occupations
- ☐   Drafters and engineering technicians
- ☐   Education, training, library, and museum occupations
- ☐   Electrical and electronic equipment mechanics, installers, and repairers
- ☐   Entertainers and performers, sports and related occupations
- ☐   Farming, fishing, and forestry occupations
- ☐   Food processing occupations
- ☐   Health diagnosing and treating occupations
- ☐   Health technologists and technicians
- ☐   Healthcare support occupations
- ☐   Information and record clerks
- ☐   Legal occupations
- ☐   Management (middle level) occupations
- ☐   Management (senior level) occupations
- ☐   Material recording, scheduling, dispatching, and distributing occupations
- ☐   Media and communications-related occupations
- ☐   Miscellaneous (installation, maintenance, and repair) occupations
- ☐   Miscellaneous (office and administrative support) occupations

☐ Miscellaneous (production) occupations
☐ Motor vehicle operators
☐ Personal care and service occupations
☐ Plant and system operators
☐ Printing occupations
☐ Protective service occupations
☐ Rail transportation occupations
☐ Sales and related occupations
☐ Scientific (life sciences) occupations
☐ Scientific (physical sciences) occupations
☐ Scientific (social sciences) occupations
☐ Vehicle and mobile equipment mechanics, installers, and repairers
☐ Water transportation occupations
☐ Other occupations

Demographic Information - Years in Your Occupation

Percent Completed: **90.2%**

Please press the Go Back *button if you want to review and/or change your response to the previous question.*

Please press the Continue *button when you are satisfied with your response.*

47. *How many years have you been engaged in your given occupation?*
(Select only one.)
☐ 1 - 11 months
☐ 1 - 2 years
☐ 3 - 5
☐ 6 - 10
☐ 11 - 20
☐ Over 20 years

Demographic Information - Major Role Played

Percent Completed: **92.2%**

Please press the Go Back *button if you want to review and/or change your response to the previous question.*

Please press the Continue *button when you are satisfied with your response.*

48. *How would you characterize the major role that you played with respect to this project?*
(Select only one.)
☐ Customer/User - A person or organization that uses the project's product.
☐ Customer Decision-Maker - A member of the customer community designated to make project decisions.
☐ Customer Representative - A member of the customer community designated as a subject matter expert.
☐ Executive Sponsor - A high ranking manager with a demonstrated interest in the project's outcome.

☐   Influencer - A person not directly related to the project's product, but can influence the course of the project.

☐   Project Director - A person with full authority, accountability, and responsibility for the project.

☐   Project Manager - The person responsible for managing the project.

☐   Project Sponsor - A person who provides financial resources in cash or kind for the project.

☐   Project Team Manager - A person directly involved in project management activities.

☐   Project Team Member - A person responsible for executing tasks and producing deliverables.

☐   Steering Committee Member - A person charged with regular or periodic oversight of the project.

Demographic Information - Age Group

Percent Completed: **94.1%**

Please press the Go Back *button if you want to review and/or change your response to the previous question.*

Please press the Continue *button when you are satisfied with your response.*

49. What is your approximate age?
(Select only one.)

☐   18 - 24 years
☐   25 - 30
☐   31 - 39
☐   40 - 49
☐   50 - 59
☐   60 - 65
☐   Over 65 years

DemographicInformation - Gender

Percent Completed: **96.1%**

Please press the Go Back *button if you want to review and/or change your response to the previous question.*

Please press the Continue *button when you are satisfied with your response.*

50. What is your gender?
(Select only one.)

☐   Male
☐   Female

Demographic Information - Additional Comments

Percent Completed: **98.0%**

Please press the Go Back *button if you want to review and/or change your response to the previous question.*

Please press the Continue *button when you are satisfied with your response.*

51. Please enter any additional comments at this time. If you have no additional comments, please press the Continue button.
  (Provide one response only.)

Thank You for Your Participation

Thank you for your participation. The data from this questionnaire will be used to analyze whether the use and results of agile software development methods provide greater customer satisfaction than the use and results of plan-driven software development methods. All of your responses will be anonymous and all data will be held in the strictest confidence. From this data, it will not be possible to distinguish specific individuals or companies. The data obtained from this questionnaire will be used in a doctoral dissertation. The results may possibly appear in an academic or trade publication. No individual responses will be revealed. To include your data in the study you must press the **Submit Your Responses** button that appears below. If you close this window, any data that you previously provided will **not** be included in the study. Again, thank you for your participation.

Percent Completed: **100.0%**

Please press the Go Back *button if you want to review your response to the previous question.*

Please press the Submit Your Responses *button when you ready to include your data in the study.*

Please close this window if you do not want your data to be included in the study.

Wissenschaftlicher Buchverlag bietet

kostenfreie

Publikation

von

wissenschaftlichen Arbeiten

Diplomarbeiten, Magisterarbeiten, Master und Bachelor Theses
sowie Dissertationen, Habilitationen und wissenschaftliche Monographien

Sie verfügen über eine wissenschaftliche Abschlußarbeit zu aktuellen oder zeitlosen
Fragestellungen, die hohen inhaltlichen und formalen Ansprüchen genügt,
und haben **Interesse an einer honorarvergüteten Publikation**?

Dann senden Sie bitte erste Informationen über Ihre Arbeit per Email
an info@vdm-verlag.de. Unser Außenlektorat meldet sich umgehend bei Ihnen.

VDM Verlag Dr. Müller Aktiengesellschaft & Co. KG
Dudweiler Landstraße 125a
D - 66123 Saarbrücken

www.vdm-verlag.de